# afternoon tea is the new happy hour

# afternoon tea is the new happy hour

gail greco

NELSON
BOOKS

An Imprint of Thomas Nelson

**Library of Congress Cataloging-in-Publication Data**

Names: Greco, Gail, author.
Title: Afternoon tea is the new happy hour : more than 75 recipes for tea, small plates, sweets & more / Gail Greco.
Description: Nashville : Nelson Books, 2023. | Summary: "Afternoon Tea Is the New Happy Hour features more than 75 recipes to make your teatime memorable.
Inside you'll find easy-to-follow recipes to create sandwiches, scones, breads, cakes, dips, and, of course-tea. This beautiful cookbook will provide you with the high-tea food ideas you can't find anywhere else"--Provided by publisher.
Identifiers: LCCN 2022040617 | ISBN 9781400334322 (hardcover) | ISBN 9781400334339 (epub)
Subjects: LCSH: Tea. | Afternoon teas. | Cooking.
Classification: LCC TX415 .G73 2023 | DDC 641.3/372--dc23/eng/20220830
LC record available at https://lccn.loc.gov/2022040617

*Printed in China*

23 24 25 26 27 GRI 6 5 4 3 2 1

*For my own "Joans of Arc" . . .*
*Joan Masker, who let the "can't" out of the bag. She has no idea how*
*significant my growth and life's successes were thanks to the gift of*
*"her" poem. (Poem on page 178.) One day in class she slipped me a*
*note, her eyes twinkling and head nodding assuredly, as if knowing she*
*was coming to my rescue. She didn't know how it would also become*
*a springboard for everything I have done and "can" do to this day.*
*Thank you, Joan, wherever you are.*

*And, I raise my teacup to my editorial muse Jone Meyer. Her*
*trusty words still linger whenever my fingertips start typing, as they*
*did for this book. "Being a writer is enduring . . . forever."*

# contents

*Introduction* ..................................................................................................ix

*Teakettle or Teapot?*..........................................................................xii

*If You Don't Have a Teakettle or Teapot* .....................................xv

*No Strings Attached: Free as a Tea Leaf*.......................................xvi

*Message In a Tea Bag: The Holy Vestment of Teas*......................xix

*Tealicious: Create Your Own Sachet of Tea* ................................xx

*Little Packets of Spice: Cooking with Tea* ..................................xxi

*Tea for Pasta Water and More*.................................................... xxii

Chapter 1: Get Your Cuppa On...................................................... 1

Chapter 2: Savory Teasers: Dips, Spreads, and Scoops................. 37

Chapter 3: Little O'Fares: Finger Foods and Tea Sandwiches ...... 77

Chapter 4: Baked to a Tea ............................................................113

*Acknowledgments*........................................................................ 177

*About the Author* ...................................................................... 179

*Index*......................................................................................... 180

# introduction

It's amazing! In just minutes, delicate tea leaves turn water into the most powerful and popular beverage in the world. Tea is a perfect drink, which explains its longevity since it was first brewed for medicinal purposes thousands of years ago. Fast forward to Britain in the Victorian era, and the occasion of tea was high tea and afternoon tea. Now, though, afternoon tea isn't just a dainty parlor event; it's taken to the streets—literally and figuratively—in the most unlikely of places.

Step right up to the bar—a bar with happy hour—and you may find friends together after a long day to "let go" over mixed non-alcoholic cold tea brews and hot tea mocktails. The Happy Hour Tea is a modern teatime with a vintage vibe that makes so much sense because it's a time-out that's chockablock with all that is delicious beverages, good food, and dear friends.

I couldn't wait to write this cookbook and create the delicious complementary teas and foods so you could hold afternoon tea as happy hour in your own home. Is it just a trend or much more? Tea is tea, right? Well, not so fast. There's actually much more to explore, beginning with the tea itself.

# the tea on tea

"Let's have a cup of tea," invites a pause. As Vietnamese monk Thich Nhat Hanh wrote, "Don't just do something, sit there"—and I'll add, "with a cup of tea." Tea offers clarity in a free-spirit way. Tea is usually described as *having a moment*, but the increasing popularity and tea trends suggest that today tea is having a renaissance. It's so popular that tea food trucks are wheeling into towns.

Today consumers want to know where their food is grown and packaged. Tea leaves are mostly from the *Camellia sinensis* evergreen bush, but their tastes vary as a result of their growing environment. The location, soil, and climate (also referred to as *terroir*) impact the assortment of tea flavors.

Tea drinkers want a natural beverage. And if you open a tea bag, you see and feel this up close. Fresh, fragrant tea shimmies out of the silk or muslin sack like undulating sands on the shore. It brings to mind an observation from Greek philosopher Aristotle. "In all things of nature there is something of the marvelous." I don't think you can get any closer to nature than drinking tea.

# a more tender bar

The health benefit of tea is one of the reasons it has become increasingly popular—especially with the millennials who are credited with starting the happy hour tea trend. Tea delivers that breathe-easy, no-worries, soothing finish—like nature that doesn't hurry and yet accomplishes everything.

Tea at happy hour serves up more savory foods with fewer and lighter sweets. And tea isn't only in a teapot, but in a cold pitcher, too, refreshing after a long day. At a bar, you may find smokier teas, like Lapsang Souchong and nitro teas (effervescence swipes any bitterness) that you can't make as easily at home.

An abundance of mouthwatering teas, including Limoncello, Raspberry Creme, and Passion Plum, have also broadened tea's passionate draw. Flowers, fruits, and healing botanicals like chamomile, ginger, and turmeric say they are teas, too, as well as new, dried wine-grape-skin teas with the flavor of chardonnay, rosè, and cabernet. Happy hour sans the hangover sounds like a perfect afternoon.

If you're unsure about how to make entertaining easier, I've included tips and suggestions to make hosting more enjoyable. If you want a more formal happy hour I've also included traditional foods, easy, fresh tea blends, and steps to help you make your own unique blend.

Theoretically, afternoon tea has always been a happy hour. I hope this book inspires you to gather with your friends and family to enjoy a cuppa.

# teakettle or teapot?

Tea should take credit for being the first to use the trendy pour-over brewing technique that coffee claims today. And like coffee, there are many ways to make tea.

A teakettle is the worker bee in the iconic stovetop tea-making method since it can withstand direct heat. Whether you're making a cup of tea in the morning or not, a teakettle is a great resource. However, since it is bulky and can be quite cumbersome to bring to the table, the teapot is a great alternative

Contrary to the classic nursery rhyme, the one way you *shouldn't* prepare water for tea is in a tea*pot*. The work described in the nursery rhyme is actually that of a steel or other heavy metal teakettle. The finer porcelain, china, or ceramic teapot isn't made for stovetop heat—even though most teapots have a lid, handle, and spout. The teapot's job is to look pretty, steep the hot water into tea, and pour.

## boil, brew, and steep

1. Regardless of whether you are using loose tea or tea bags, always add cold filtered water to the teakettle.
2. Over high heat, bring water to a brisk steaming. For some teas that might be just before or just to the boil. Check tea's packaging for the advised temperature; it depends on the leaves and how long they take to unfurl their essence.
3. While the water heats up, run hot tap water into the teapot to warm it up.
4. Add your tea bag, or for loose tea, fill the tea infuser loosely, about one teaspoon

per six ounces of water and then one extra for the pot. Add the infuser to the teapot. It's important to note that teas such as white and oolong may call for more than a teaspoon per cup.

5. As soon as the water is ready, pour from the kettle into the teapot.
6. Allow the tea to steep at least five minutes or as suggested. Steeping begins as the water is poured over the tea.

# if you don't have a teakettle or teapot

Boiling water in a saucepan is an option when you don't have a teakettle. You can drop the leaves or tea bags into the pan, steep, strain, and serve. When boiling water in a saucepan keep an eye on the pot to make sure the water doesn't boil over.

One of my favorite ways to prepare loose tea is to steep it in a French press coffee and teamaker. Scoop the tea into the press and then pour in the hot water. Position the plunger at the top of the pot and watch the water turn to tea after several minutes. Press the filter down and the tea is ready to serve.

# no strings attached:
# free as a tea leaf

Fresh tea leaves require a couple more steps when it comes to preparation. But they are worth it because of their incomparable flavor. As the leaves absorb water, they open, dispensing incredible, clear tasting, crisp flavor.

A tea strainer is the main tool needed when brewing loose tea leaves. Fine-mesh tea-steeping strainers come in varying sizes for fitting over or into cups. Some teapots have built-in tea strainers—making it even easier.

Once I'm finished with my tea, I often drop the spent leaves into my flower beds to nourish plants, or chop them finely so I can cook with them. Damp tea leaves also work as a great odor eliminator for your wooden cutting board. Using your fingers, rub the leaves into the wood. Then rinse and dry.

# message in a tea bag: the holy vestment of teas

Tea bags—also called tea sacks or sachets—were invented in the early twentieth century. They come in a pageant of shapes—with and without strings—and some tea companies even print inspirational quotes and messages on their paper tea tags. (Today my tea tag said, "Just when the caterpillar thought the world was over, it became a butterfly.")

Steeping times are recommended to make a perfectly balanced cuppa, otherwise the tea turns bitter if it's steeped too long and bland if not long enough. Avoid squeezing tea bags because it can cause acidity.

Tea bags are often the best option for a big party, if you're in a hurry, or whenever loose tea is not practical. When serving a crowd, making tea with individual tea bags gets even easier if you use a clean drip coffeemaker. Place six to eight tea bags in the filter basket, depending on the type of tea. Add twelve cups of water to the reservoir, turn on the machine, and let it drip into the carafe. Piece of (tea) cake!

# tealicious: create your own sachet of tea

Although there are master tea blenders, you don't have to be an impresario to build your own little tea type. In fact, once you've created your own tea blend share it with your guests at your next teatime and let everyone help you name your blend.

To create your own tea blend, start with a base tea, such as black, green, white, oolong, or pu-erh. These basic teas produce familiar blends like Earl Grey, Ceylon, English Breakfast, and Darjeeling.

Use your sense of smell as a guide to help mix basic teas and add in dried herbs, edible flowers, and fruit bits. When combining the teas measure a generous table-spoon or two into an empty mesh bag. Tea filter bags are available online in a variety of sizes. Keep in mind, the leaves can be challenging to measure when you're dealing with such a small amount. I suggest measuring on a pinch method when you're creating the tea. Once you have the basic recipe down, you can measure it out for future blending.

Making a tea blend from two tablespoons of fresh herbs is another option for a tea bag, and this is often a hit at the tea table since it's so unexpected. Tea-goers dip the tea bag into their cup and the fragrance of the herbs is delightful. You can make these tea bags in advance and store in a covered container in the fridge.

# little packets of spice: cooking with tea

Tea leaves are not just for steeping into a delicious beverage; you can also eat them by using a nut grinder and grinding them into a powder. The powder should be stored in fresh, empty tea bags and sealed in a tin for later use. There are many ways you can use the tea leaf powder in your everyday cooking. You can:

- Sprinkle into a garden salad like you would salt and pepper.
- Enhance the flavor for pancake batter, scones, and granola.
- Use as a meat rub, or as a crust for chicken or fish.
- Add a teaspoon of powdered Earl Grey tea to your scrambled eggs. The bergamot in this classic black tea gives the breakfast entree a citrusy zing.

Determine which teas work with which foods just as you would with any other condiments.

# tea for pasta water
# and more

Always keep a pitcher of tea readily available in the fridge because you can always substitute tea for water. I use this substitute to jazz up my cooking , particularly in soups, when cooking dried beans, and when boiling pasta. Brewed tea can be used in a marinade, sauce, or a glaze, depending on your recipe.

Smoky teas are great to use in cooking. The smoking happens naturally when the leaves are roasted during the drying process as in the famous Lapsang Souchong tea, which is often just called smoked tea. This tea is processed over pine or cypress so the smoke penetrates the tea, imparting the wonderful woodsy aroma.

## Chapter 1

# get your cuppa on

As simple as tea is, it's also complex, but joyfully so! The market is saturated with tea types blended by professional tea masters or sommeliers, producing nuanced flavors that are scrumptious. Tea is not just something to taste. You can feel it too.

It's a great time to be a tea lover. Happy hour doesn't need to involve alcoholic beverages because afternoon tea is the new happy hour. I refer to tea cocktails as *mockteals*. If you do choose to partake in mockteal drinking, you need to try a cup of pu-erh tea. The pu-erh tea is aged and fermented, making it great for your digestive system.

With all the tea choices, knowing the tea basics will help you decide what to serve in your *cuppa*. A cuppa is an endearing reference to a cup of tea or coffee in a teacup, mug, glass, or any drinking vessel. The tea plant and how its leaves are processed determine the tea that ends up in your cuppa. The same is true with herbal teas—also called elixirs or tisanes—made up of herbs, roots, barks, seeds, or fruits. There are a large variety of teas available and the benefits of true teas are fascinating.

Some varieties of tea have disease-fighting antioxidants and polyphenols that have been known to transform moods and create a more positive mindset. The antioxidants slow down caffeine absorption so there's no rush or crash effect. Aside from the recipes I've included, there are so many great tea choices available. I encourage you to dig deeper on your own!

# more tea choices

## yerba mate

This is a crisp, earthy-tasting tea from South America that you can brew in hot water or buy in prepackaged cans. Yerba Mate is enormously popular with happy hour tea-goers because it has more of a boozy buzz than other teas.

## matcha tea

Powdered matcha tea is a foamy tea that tastes great with almond or coconut milk, and powdered cacao or chocolate. You can foam it up with a special Japanese bamboo chasen (whisk) or any small wire whisk.

## kombucha tea

A non-alcoholic black or green fermented tea drink, kombucha is lightly effervescent and available in different flavors at grocery stores and on tap at some bars.

## peppermint tea

Some herbal teas like peppermint tea are invigorating without any caffeine. When you feel tired or groggy you'll be surprised how peppermint tea can provide you with a lift. It's one of my favorites.

## the zest is yet to come: tea stirrings

What you stir into a basic tea affects the flavor. Milk, for example, is better than heavy cream because it will not drastically change the tea. However, nut, soy, almond, or coconut milk will.

A squirt of lemon is okay if you're in the mood for a refresh. I use Meyer lemons when they are in season because they are less acidic and more floral than most lemons.

Speaking of lemons, lime and orange peels imbue hot tea with a delightful essence, since their natural oils are in the fruit's skin. When using lime and orange peels, steep the peels with the tea. Then strain and discard or dry for other desired uses.

# sweeteners

- Adding sweeteners to tea foils any bitter tea edge. *"Gimme some sugar"* is sweet talk for *"I need a hug or a kiss."* But when that's not possible, find it in your tea with an assortment of specialty sugars. Be mindful that any syrups or liqueurs will change the basic tea taste—so add something complementary.
- White and cane sugars are the most popular for tea. Substitute sweeteners are agave, stevia, and monk fruit.
- Turbinado sugar, not as fine in texture as white sugar, complements the earthiness of tea with a molasses finish.
- Rock sugar is fun at happy hour tea since it's so visual. Rock sugar is made from beet or cane sugar, is amber in color, and comes in the shape of glistening nuggets.
- Honey is tea's best friend as long as you don't add too much since its own flavor can eclipse that of the tea's.
- For a smoky accent, there are bourbon-soaked sugars to give the tea a more woodsy, leathery flavor.
- Adding a quarter teaspoon of vanilla extract in a cup perfumes the tea with an almost marshmallowy essence. Speaking of 'mallows, float a few minis in a teacup. Floating marshmallows are like sprinkles on a cupcake—guaranteed to turn frowns into smiles.
- Stir a teaspoon of fruit preserves into a basic black tea.
- A touch of date syrup is a great tea sweetener. It is processed with only dates and water into a caramel liquid, so it never masks flavor.

# the serve

- A crown jewel of afternoon tea is a bone china pinky pointer teacup. This teacup is designed with a wide top to cool tea for sipping. Porcelain straight-sided modern bone china mugs are dainty but less formal for everyday use. A mug is also appropriate for tea, especially at happy hour. Its narrow shaft has the advantage of funneling tea's aroma while enhancing each sip with fragrance.
- Even a casual tea can be served with delicate teacups as their appearance alone is calming. Don't worry if your teacups don't match—each one has a story. It can be fun to scour antique shops and garage sales for unique, mismatched teacups. They also make great caddies for nuts, tea bags, and sweeteners.
- The happy hour tea might involve a lot of mingling and conversation, so slimmer drinking glasses for iced teas, champagne teas, or room temp teas are ideal since they're easier to hold.
- Fruit preserve jars are heftier than most teacups for a more casual, fun teatime or a happy hour tea mockteal or latte.
- To serve cream with dessert, the true Devonshire unpasteurized cream is an afternoon tea tradition. When it's not available, I substitute with the rich, nutty taste of cultured crème fraiche.
- Hosting and serving a tea tasting (like a wine tasting) with four to six different teas is a fun way guests can experiment with different blends.

# hot teas

*Traditional afternoon tea is mostly about hot teas, and they also work for happy hour as a soothing drink to start off with. Brew ahead of time and keep warm in a carafe. Hot tea is also versatile and can easily be turned into iced tea.*

Apple Hibiscus Tea

Ginger Date Tea

Five o'clock High Tea Mockteal

Basic Barista Tea Latte with Rooibos

Earl Grey Vanilla Almond Milk Latte

Chocolate Mint and Coconut Tea Latte

# apple hibiscus tea

Makes: 6 to 8 servings

*Hot or cold, this tea is a crisp complement to savory appetizers.*

8 hibiscus tea bags
2 cups boiling water
2 teaspoons honey

4 cups pure (not from
    concentrate) unsweetened
    apple juice

1. Place the tea bags in a teapot with boiling water and steep 5 minutes.

2. Squeeze excess tea from tea bags and discard.

3. Stir in honey until melted throughout.

4. Stir in apple juice.

5. Serve in individual teacups.

# ginger date tea

Makes: 2 servings

*Use fresh ginger root to enhance this botanical tea by boiling ginger until it releases the slightly peppery-sweet aroma. It's great for any tea party or middle-of-the-day pick-me-up.*

2 tablespoons shaved fresh ginger root
4 cups water

Fresh juice from half of a lemon
1 generous tablespoon date syrup

1. Place ginger and water in a medium saucepan and bring to a boil.

2. Lower heat to medium-low and simmer for 15 to 20 minutes or until liquid becomes fragrant.

3. Strain and stir in the lemon juice and date syrup and serve.

# five o'clock high tea mockteal

## Makes: 8 servings

*Lavender and chamomile's calming properties
are well-suited for tea late in the day.*

8 cups water
1/4 cup fresh culinary (not craft)
   lavender buds
2 tablespoons loose
   chamomile leaves and bud

1 tablespoon vanilla extract
Choice of sweetener, if
   desired

1. Bring the water to a full boil.

2. Once boiled, transfer boiled water to a teapot.

3. Place the lavender and chamomile into the teapot and steep for
   10 to 12 minutes.

4. Stir in the vanilla.

5. Pour the tea into cups through a strainer and serve with your choice of
   sweetener.

# basic barista tea latte with rooibos

## Makes: 2 servings

*If you don't have a frother, vigorously whisk the milk in a saucepan over medium heat until it forms a bubbly lather.*

½ cup water
2 rooibos tea bags
1 ½ cups milk, frothed

2 teaspoons sugar
Ground cinnamon or candied
   sprinkles for garnish

1. Boil the water and divide it between 2 mugs.

2. Place a tea bag in each mug and steep for at least 5 minutes.

3. While steeping, froth the milk and set aside.

4. Squeeze tea bags and remove.

5. Stir in the sugar.

6. Dollop the thick, frothy milk overtop.

7. Dust with colorful candy sprinkles or ground cinnamon. Serve warm or at room temperature.

# earl grey vanilla almond milk latte

### Makes: 8 to 10 servings

*The hint of bergamot spice in the Earl Grey gives this latte a
sweet kick. To froth almond milk, heat it up before whisking.*

2 cups unsweetened vanilla
  almond milk
1 teaspoon vanilla extract
1 teaspoon cinnamon
1/2 teaspoon cardamom
1 teaspoon ground almonds,
  more for garnish

1/3 cup honey
1 quart filtered water
8 teaspoons Earl Grey tea
  leaves
Whipped cream or frothed
  almond milk, for topping

1. In a medium saucepan over medium-low heat, heat almond milk with
   the vanilla extract, cinnamon, cardamom, almonds, and honey. Simmer
   for 30 minutes, stirring often.

2. Boil the water in a teakettle or pot with lid.

3. Remove boiling water from heat and add the tea leaves. Steep 6 minutes
   and strain into a pitcher.

4. Add the almond milk mixture to the pitcher and stir well as you pour.

5. Serve topped with whipped cream or frothed almond milk.

# chocolate mint and coconut tea latte

## Makes: 2 servings

*Top this with a mint sprig per cup, for a lively look and fragrance. Mugs (rather than delicate teacups) are a better choice for serving a latte.*

1 cup water
2 teaspoons fresh peppermint
  or other mint tea leaves
4 sprigs fresh mint, plus a few
  leaves for garnish

1½ cups coconut milk
1 teaspoon sugar, divided
2 tablespoons dark chocolate
  syrup, divided

1. Boil water in a small saucepan and stir in tea and fresh mint sprigs.

2. Steep tea for at least 5 minutes.

3. While steeping, froth the coconut milk and set aside.

4. Pour the tea through a strainer into 2 mugs.

5. Stir sugar into each cup, followed by the chocolate syrup.

6. Slowly fold in the frothed coconut milk and serve.

# cold brews, iced teas, and cool spirits

*Unlike iced tea, cold brew tea is prepared by infusing tea in cold water. The result is a smoother, less bitter, balanced tea since fewer bitter tannins are released.*

*Cold brew can be made with tea bags or loose leaves, and some packagers are now selling specific cold brew instant tea bags. The longer you let the brew steep, the stronger the flavor. If you're short on time, use tea ice cubes to intensify the brew.*

Lemony Cream Sherry Iced Tea

Fruity Herbal Iced Tea Sparkler

Alice's Sorbet Float Tea

Salted Caramel Cold Brew Milk Tea

Happy Hour Muddled-Mint Tea Cocktail

Chilled Wine Tea

Spiked Peach and Coconut Tea Grog

Tea Toddy One-Shot

# lemony cream sherry iced tea

Makes: 10 to 12 servings

*Big people's lemonade with tea and a little spirit!*

4 Orange Pekoe tea bags
1 quart boiling water
Juice of 6 medium lemons
1 pint cold filtered water

3 cinnamon sticks
1 cup sugar
2 cups cream sherry

1. Steep the tea in boiling water for 15 minutes to concentrate the tea.

2. Transfer to a medium saucepan and add the lemon juice, cold water, and cinnamon sticks.

3. Bring to a boil and then turn down to a simmer for 5 minutes.

4. Remove the cinnamon sticks and stir in the sugar until dissolved.

5. Pour into a pitcher and chill in the fridge.

6. Just before serving, stir in the sherry and serve.

# fruity herbal iced tea sparkler

## Makes: 8 to 10 servings

*Rooibos, sage, rose hips, or holy basil (Tulsi) herbs are a good choice
for the tea enlivened by the sparkling addition. A substitute for
the Prosecco is sparkling water, but adjust the sugar to taste.*

2 oranges
2 medium lemons
1 (16 ounce) can frozen apple
   juice concentrate, thawed

3 cups brewed herbal tea of
   choice, such as Tulsi
1/3 cup sugar
2 cups Prosecco
Thyme sprigs, for garnish

1. Juice 1 of the oranges and 1 of the lemons and stir the juice into a large pitcher with the apple juice concentrate and herbal tea.

2. Cut the remaining orange and lemon into thin slices and place in a bowl with the sugar, pressing the sweetener into the fruits with the back of a wooden spoon.

3. Add sugared fruit slices to the pitcher and stir.

4. Pour in the Prosecco and add to glasses with ice and serve.

5. Rub a thyme sprig around the top edge of the glass and use as a stirrer—float in the glass for some added zing!

# alice's sorbet float tea

## Makes: 8 servings

*Cold tea is full of imagination in this recipe as was the tea party down the Rabbit Hole in Wonderland. But this dip makes sense with the sorbet used as an icy sweetener to the fresh, herbal, grassy flavor of the Sencha. No ice cubes needed.*

8 Sencha tea bags
1 cup heavy cream

8 small scoops (about 1 pint) black cherry or raspberry sorbet

1. Brew tea for 12 minutes.

2. Place in the fridge until chilled.

3. Stir in heavy cream and top each serving with a scoop of the sorbet. Serve immediately.

# salted caramel cold brew milk tea

### Makes: 2 servings

*Tea is usually steeped in water, but any liquid can make
an infused cold brew. My favorite is milk.*

2 cups whole milk
¼ cup loose black tea of
   choice, such as Orange
   Pekoe

2 tablespoons caramel sauce
½ teaspoon finely granulated
   salt

1. Add milk to a saucepan and stir in the tea, caramel, and salt.

2. Heat on medium-low, simmering for about 10 minutes. Do not bring
   to a boil.

3. Remove from the heat and pour through a strainer into a pitcher.

4. Chill in the fridge for at least an hour before serving.

# happy hour muddled-mint tea cocktail

Makes: 4 servings

*Make this a day ahead of serving to infuse the mint and berries.
You can serve a full glass of this cocktail or just a taste.*

2 tablespoons honey
1½ cups brewed room-temp
  (not chilled) hibiscus or
  jasmine tea
¾ cup strawberry juice (about
  1 pint berries, juiced)

½ bunch fresh and fragrant
  mint sprigs
4 medium strawberries, sliced
1½ cups Rosè Prosecco
  (substitute ginger ale)

1.  Add honey to the bottom of a clear pitcher and stir in the tea until the honey is no longer clumpy.

2.  Stir in the strawberry juice, mixing well.

3.  Drop in the mint and, using a wooden spoon, press (muddle) the leaves against the sides of the pitcher to release the oil essence from the mint.

4.  Drop in the strawberries. Cover and let sit in the fridge overnight.

5.  When ready to serve, remove mint and berries and divide drink among the glasses.

6.  Top with Prosecco and serve.

# chilled wine tea

Makes: 2 to 4 servings

*Wine tea is perfect for a happy hour teatime. Some companies are selling dried grape skins in tea bags to taste like wine without the alcoholic content. A nice idea! Others are offering teas with wine flavoring. A substitute in this recipe is berry-flavored tea like hibiscus.*

1 cup brewed wine tea (white or red)

1/2 cup berry cocktail syrup
1 cup Riesling (optional)

1. Brew tea and chill.

2. Stir in the syrup and evenly divide among the glasses.

3. Add ice, top with wine (optional), and serve.

# spiked peach and coconut tea grog

## Makes: 4 to 6 servings

*Using coconut milk instead of water makes this a more updated grog.*

2 cups fresh peaches, pitted, skinned, and coarsely chopped
1 cup vodka
1 cup peach nectar

½ cup coconut milk
1½ cups brewed mango or other fruity brewed tea of choice
Fruit for garnish (optional)

1. Place the peaches and vodka in a food processor or large blender and process until smooth. (It will be thick.)

2. Add nectar, milk, and fruit tea and blend until smooth.

3. Pour into glasses and garnish with fruit if desired.

# tea toddy one-shot

Makes: 6 servings

*A fun way to open the happy hour tea at home with a toast. Substitute chai or green tea. Serve in shot glasses or mini copper mules and top with whipped cream, if desired.*

6 teaspoons loose black tea leaves
½ teaspoon ground cloves

3 cups boiling filtered water
3 teaspoons rum

1. Place the tea and cloves in a small saucepan.

2. Add 1 cup of the boiling water.

3. Steep 5 minutes and then, using a strainer, pour a few tablespoons of the concentrated tea into 6 shot glass-sized cups.

4. Fill each cup evenly with the remaining water.

5. Top each with a splash of rum and serve.

Chapter 2

# savory teasers:
# dips, spreads, and scoops

Planning and hosting teatime shouldn't feel overwhelming. A casual happy hour tea can be as simple as offering a spread and letting your guests take it from there. And that's where the teatime grazing board comes in. Tea-goers are invited to fill their plates at their own pace, picking and choosing from the board as they mingle with friends.

The grazing board makes party planning simple because foods complement each other with their natural colors, textures, patterns, and flavors.

A large wood cutting board provides a basic blank canvas, but an artistic tray or board is a fun way to keep the spread unique and serves as a great conversation starter. As food disappears from the tray, a pretty design emerges so nothing looks picked over. You can add a thin turntable underneath the board for easy access around the tea table.

It's important to note that these food boards are not charcuterie boards. Restaurants recently introduced the French custom of serving cured meat, cheese, and a condiment on a board as a menu item. The idea caught on quickly with home entertainers filling boards with all kinds of foods and loosely referring to them as charcuterie boards. Tea drinkers refer to these delicious trays as food grazing boards.

# dips

Spicy Baked Artichoke Bruschetta

Buffalo Hot Chicken Dip

Baked Ricotta Dip

Whipped Feta Dip

Cheddar Ranch Crab Dip

Lemony Smoked Trout

White Bean "Hummus"

# spicy baked artichoke bruschetta

### Makes: About 2 cups

*Serve warm with thinly sliced toasted French bread. The dressing gives this artichoke dip a slightly tomato tang.*

1 (15-ounce) can (not in oil) artichoke hearts, drained
½ cup drained small-curd cottage cheese
⅓ cup mayonnaise
¼ cup plus 2 tablespoons Thousand Island dressing

1 cup finely grated Parmesan cheese, divided
1 ½ teaspoons Worcestershire sauce
Dash of hot sauce (optional)

1. Preheat oven to 350ºF.

2. Place artichokes in the food processor and pulse several times to chop.

3. Add cottage cheese, mayo, dressing, ¾ cup of the cheese, and Worcestershire.

4. Whisk to combine. Taste and add hot sauce if desired.

5. Transfer to a small ovenproof bowl and sprinkle with remaining cheese.

6. Bake for 20 to 30 minutes or until light brown on top.

# buffalo hot chicken dip

Makes: 4 cups

*Serve this with crisp fresh veggies or dollop into
the Savory Thumbprint Cookie Cups.*

½ cup plain Greek yogurt
8 ounces whipped cream
 cheese
1 (1 oz.) package ranch
 seasoning
4 slices cooked bacon, finely
 chopped

1 small bunch (about 8) green
 onions, coarsely chopped
2 tablespoons hot sauce (or
 more to taste)
2 cups cooked white chicken
 breast meat, shredded
½ cup plus 2 tablespoons
 Monterey Jack cheese

1. Preheat oven to 350°F.

2. In a medium mixing bowl combine yogurt, cream cheese, and ranch
   seasoning.

3. Fold in bacon bits and onions, leaving a handful for garnishing.

4. Stir in hot sauce. Taste and adjust to your level of desired spiciness.

5. Fold in chicken and ½ cup of the cheese.

6. Pour chicken mixture into a 1-quart baking dish.

7. Bake 10 minutes and evenly top with remaining onions and cheese.

8. Bake an additional 10 minutes to warm through and melt the cheese.

# baked ricotta dip

Makes: 1 ½ cups

*The lemon addition to the ricotta adds a brightness to
the palate. Dig in with crackers or crudites.
Dollop onto crusty bread or smear onto flatbread—
it's also delicious as a base for pizza.*

1 pound whole-milk ricotta
cheese
Zest of 1 lemon
1 teaspoon dried garlic flakes
½ teaspoon salt, plus more for
sprinkling

2 tablespoons shredded
Pecorino Romano cheese
2 teaspoons mixed dried
Italian herbs, plus more for
sprinkling
Fresh cracked pepper
Olive oil for drizzling

1. Preheat oven to 400°F.

2. Drain ricotta of any water and transfer to a bowl.

3. Whisk lemon zest, garlic flakes, and ½ teaspoon of the salt into ricotta.

4. Pour mixture into a shallow 2-cup ovenproof dish.

5. Top with the shredded cheese, herbs, and a few twists of pepper.

6. Bake 15 to 20 minutes until cheese is bubbly and a light golden brown.

7. Cool to room temp before serving. Drizzle with olive oil and a pinch of
   salt and herbs if desired.

# whipped feta dip

Makes: 1 cup

*A tasty dip for crudites or to spread on a tea sandwich.
Roasted peppers make a handy condiment to keep in your
fridge for many everyday uses, from salads to pasta.*

4 ounces crumbled feta
  cheese
4 ounces crème fraiche
2 tablespoons olive oil

1 teaspoon fresh lemon juice
2 tablespoons finely chopped
  roasted peppers
1/2 teaspoon sugar

**1.** Combine feta, crème fraiche, olive oil, lemon juice, peppers, and sugar
in a food processor and blend for approximately 20 seconds.

**2.** Stop and scrape sides of bowl and continue blending until smooth.

**3.** Serve immediately or store in fridge in an airtight container.

# cheddar ranch crab dip

## Makes: 4 cups

*Great served on crackers, or as a fun alternative place a spoonful of dip on large lettuce leaves, roll, and serve on a platter.*

2 cups fresh lump or backfin crab meat
2 tablespoons finely chopped fresh chives
4 ounces whipped cream cheese
½ cup mayonnaise
½ cup ranch-style dressing

1 tablespoon fresh lemon juice
1 teaspoon Worcestershire sauce
½ teaspoon hot sauce
1 cup shredded aged Cheddar cheese
Salt and pepper

1. Crumble crab meat in a medium mixing bowl and stir in chives. Set aside.

2. In a large bowl, whisk together cream cheese, mayonnaise, ranch dressing, lemon juice, Worcestershire, and hot sauce until thoroughly combined.

3. Pour in the crab meat and fold in the cheese.

4. Add salt and pepper to taste. Refrigerate in an airtight container for a couple of hours before serving.

# lemony smoked trout

## Makes: 1 cup

*You can buy smoked trout in the seafood department, but canned smoked trout is available in the tuna section. I love the Trader Joe's brand of skinless smoked trout fillets.*

4 ounces smoked trout, drained (if canned)

4 ounces cream cheese

2 tablespoons dried onion

A few sprigs of fresh chopped dill

2 drops or so Worcestershire sauce

1 tablespoon grated lemon zest

1 tablespoon fresh lemon juice

1/4 teaspoon hot sauce

1. Using a fork, flake the trout into small pieces and set aside.

2. In a medium mixing bowl, beat the cream cheese, onion, dill, Worcestershire, lemon zest, lemon juice, and hot sauce with a hand mixer until smooth.

3. Fold in the trout.

4. Place in a bowl and serve.

# white bean "hummus"

## Makes: 2 cups

*Instead of chickpeas, I use white beans for a no-fuss alternative since you don't have to slough the skin off each bean. I also think the taste and texture of the white beans are more interesting.*

1 (15-ounce) can white
   cannellini beans, drained,
   reserving ¼ cup liquid
1 clove garlic, finely chopped
¼ cup sesame tahini
¼ cup olive oil

¼ cup fresh lemon juice
1 teaspoon cumin
1 teaspoon chili seasoning
Salt and pepper
Olive oil for drizzling

1. Combine beans and garlic in a food processor and pulse to break up.

2. Add tahini, olive oil, and lemon juice and process to blend.

3. Add cumin and chili seasoning. Process for approximately 2 minutes or until the mixture is smooth. (Add some reserved bean liquid if mixture is too dry.)

4. Taste. Add salt and pepper if desired.

5. Refrigerate and when ready to serve at room temp, sprinkle a little olive oil on top.

# spreads

Maple and Bacon Onion Jam

Lemon Aioli

Red Cherry Relish

Toasted Walnut Microgreens Pesto

Rum Raisin Cheddar Spread

Ranch-Style Cucumber Spread

Baked Mushroom Patè

Sundried Tomato Creamy Cheese

# maple and bacon onion jam

## Makes: About 2 cups

*Sweet maple and salty bacon combine to make up this perfect pantry condiment for many appetizers such as soups, cooked chicken, or fish. Serve with crackers or dollop into the Savory Thumbprint Cookie Cups.*

1 pound smoky bacon slices
4 cups thinly sliced red onion
2 tablespoons light brown
   sugar

¼ cup maple syrup
¼ cup apple cider vinegar
Pinch of black pepper

1. In a large skillet, cook the bacon until crispy but still tender.

2. Drain bacon on a paper towel. Cut into tiny bits and set aside.

3. Leave approximately ¼ cup of bacon fat in the pan. Add onions and cook over medium-low heat for 20 to 30 minutes—stirring often until onions are limp and caramelized.

4. Remove and coarsely chop, then return to the pan.

5. Stir in brown sugar, syrup, and vinegar. Lower heat to simmer the mixture for 8 to 10 minutes to thicken.

6. Add black pepper to taste.

7. Store in a lidded jar in the fridge until ready to use.

# lemon aioli

## Makes: 3/4 cup

*This is a nice all-around dipper for spicy little
bites or as a spread for sandwiches.*

4 ounces plain Greek yogurt
2 cloves garlic, minced
Zest of 1 small lemon
1 tablespoon fresh lemon juice

1 heaping teaspoon olive oil
1 heaping tablespoon honey
Salt and pepper to taste

1. In a small bowl, whisk together yogurt, garlic, lemon zest and juice, olive oil, and honey.

2. Taste and season with salt and pepper as desired.

# red cherry relish

Makes: 2 ½ cups

*This relish has a tangy and sweet taste. You can combine this with your favorite egg salad for a delicious tea sandwich or place on top of cheese. Pairs well with basic hot or cold teas.*

2 tablespoons avocado oil
2 cups coarsely chopped stemmed and pitted red cherries

¾ cup minced red onion
¾ cup red wine vinegar

1. Heat oil in a medium saucepan.

2. Add cherries and onions and sauté for 6 to 8 minutes until softened.

3. Stir in vinegar and cook, reducing the vinegar enough to thicken the mix.

4. Remove from heat. Cool and serve or store in fridge until ready to serve.

# toasted walnut microgreens pesto

Makes: 1 cup

*The delicate flavor of healthy microgreens complements herbal teas. Use as a dip for potato wedges, spread on tea sandwiches, or mix the pesto into your favorite pasta.*

1/3 cup walnut pieces
1/4 cup finely chopped red onion
2 cups mixed microgreens such as arugula, kale, radish, red amaranth
Grated zest of 1/2 lemon

1 tablespoon fresh lemon juice
1 teaspoon salt
1/2 teaspoon ground black pepper
3/4 cup grated Parmesan cheese
3/4 cup olive oil

1. Add walnuts to a small skillet and toast over medium heat. Stir often. Keep a close watch because they can burn quickly, but you'll know they are ready when fragrant.

2. Remove from pan and cool.

3. In a food processor, pulse the nuts with the onions until finely chopped.

4. Pulse in the microgreens, lemon zest and juice, salt, pepper, and cheese until blended.

5. While processor is running, slowly add olive oil and run processor until smooth. Mixture should have the consistency of a spread. Add more olive oil if too dry.

# rum raisin cheddar spread

Makes: 1 ½ cups

*Soaking the raisins in the rum creates the best flavor, but if you prefer, swap out the rum and soak raisins in a double-strength brew of rooibos tea that echoes the nutty flavor of the rum.*

1 cup raisins
⅓ cup rum

1 cup shredded sharp Cheddar cheese
6 ounces cream cheese

1. Soak raisins in rum for 1 hour or more, until plump.

2. Meanwhile, in a food processor, combine the Cheddar and cream cheese until smooth.

3. Add in the soaked raisins and rum and mix until well blended.

4. Serve or store in an airtight container in the fridge.

# ranch-style cucumber spread

## Makes: 2 cups

*Delicious on rye toast or water crackers.*

½ cup cream cheese, softened
½ cup mayonnaise
¼ cup sour cream
¼ cup ranch salad dressing
¼ teaspoon chopped fresh
  parsley

¼ teaspoon chopped fresh
  basil
½ teaspoon salt
½ teaspoon black pepper
½ cup peeled, seeded, and
  finely diced cucumbers

1. In a large mixing bowl, whisk together cream cheese, mayo, sour cream, dressing, parsley, basil, salt, and pepper until creamy.

2. Fold in the cucumbers and refrigerate two hours before serving.

# baked mushroom patè

## Makes: 1 patè loaf (approximately 3 cups)

*Serve this as a sliced loaf on a plate and dig in with your choice of scoopers. This can be made ahead of time or frozen, thawed, and served at room temp.*

2 tablespoons butter
1½ pounds baby portobello mushrooms, coarsely chopped
½ pound shiitake mushrooms (stems removed), coarsely chopped
2 small shallots, finely chopped
2 tablespoons Dijon-style mustard

1 tablespoon minced fresh garlic
1 tablespoon dried tarragon
½ teaspoon salt
½ teaspoon ground black pepper
1 cup coarsely shredded Swiss cheese
8 ounces cream cheese, softened
6 egg whites

1. Preheat oven to 375°F.

2. Heat butter in a medium skillet over medium heat.

3. Sauté mushrooms and shallots until soft.

4. Stir in the mustard, garlic, tarragon, salt, and pepper, mixing well.

5. Fold in the Swiss cheese and cream cheese and let them melt a bit.

6. Transfer the mix to a food processor and puree until smooth.

7. One at a time, process in the egg whites.

8. Transfer mix to a well-greased 9 x 5-inch loaf pan. Place the loaf pan into a larger baking pan. Pour water halfway up the sides of the loaf pan.

**9.** Cover both pans with foil and bake in the oven for 1 hour or until tester comes out clean. Cool on a wire rack. Release from pan and place on a serving plate with crackers or toast points.

# sundried tomato creamy cheese

Makes: 1 1/2 cups

*You can substitute the Italian herbs for any desired blend and change up the taste a bit with the Italian sheep's grating cheese instead of Parmesan.*

1/2 cup oil-packed sundried
  tomatoes
8 ounces cream cheese
1/4 cup (1/2 stick) butter
1/2 cup grated Pecorino
  Romano cheese

1 clove garlic, finely grated
1/4 teaspoon dried rosemary
1/4 teaspoon dried oregano
1/4 teaspoon dried basil

1. Combine tomatoes, cream cheese, butter, Pecorino Romano, garlic, rosemary, oregano, and basil in a food processor. Pause occasionally to scrape sides of the bowl—the mixture may be thick.

2. Transfer to an airtight container and refrigerate 2 hours to set before serving.

# scoops

*Crackers, thin toast points, raw veggies, cooked shrimp, and apple slices are great options for scooping dips and spreads, but here are few of the more unusual that are worth the effort for a creative tea table.*

Savory Thumbprint Cookie Cups

Roasted Delicata Squash Dippers

Mini Soft Baked Pretzels

Roasted Sweet Potato Wedges

# savory thumbprint cookie cups

### Makes: Approximately 2 dozen

*Usually filled with jam, these cookies take on the role of a cracker, but better! After they are baked, the iconic concave thumbprint (divot) can be filled with any dip. Quite a conversation starter at the tea table.*

½ cup (1 stick) butter, softened
2 scant tablespoons superfine
   sugar to balance flavors, not
   sweeten
¼ teaspoon salt

⅓ cup finely grated Pecorino
   Romano cheese
2 egg yolks
2 teaspoons powdered green
   or rooibos tea*
1 cup all-purpose flour

1. Preheat oven to 350°F.

2. In a large bowl, mix the butter with an electric mixer until smooth.

3. Add sugar, salt, and cheese. Mix until combined.

4. Mix in egg yolks and tea.

5. Slowly add flour until dough forms.

6. Working with lightly floured hands, roll dough into 1-inch balls and place ½ inch apart on a baking sheet.

7. Using your thumb or a rounded measuring spoon (bottom dipped in flour to keep from sticking), press into the center of each ball to create a well.

8. Bake 15 minutes or until bottoms start to turn golden brown.

9. Remove from the oven and place pan on a wire rack for 2 minutes. (Note: If cookies puff, lightly press spoon into them again while still warm).

**10.** Remove cookies to the rack to continue cooling.

*\* As discussed in chapter 1, create powdered tea—loose or from tea bags—in a nut grinder. Or, if you must, substitute the tea with dried herbs.*

# roasted delicata squash dippers

## Makes: 3 to 4 cups

*Delicate as its name implies, this is a sweet, buttery veggie with a healthy, earthy edge that can be served with a variety of dips.*

1 medium-sized delicata squash

1½ tablespoons sunflower oil

1 tablespoon dried Italian herb mix

1. Preheat oven to 400°F.

2. Wash outside of squash. Cut off ends and discard, then cut in half lengthwise.

3. Using a soup spoon, scrape out the seeds and stringy pulp.

4. Turn flesh-side down on a cutting board and cut into ¼-inch half-moon shapes.

5. In a large bowl, drizzle the oil over the slices to coat well.

6. Toss with the herbs.

7. Place slices on a nonstick baking pan or cookie sheet.

8. Bake 20 minutes, flipping over halfway through and roasting until golden brown.

9. Remove from oven and cool on wire rack.

# mini soft baked pretzels

### Makes: 10 to 16 depending on size

*We've made these smaller for dipping. Boiling the pretzels puffs them up, making the insides chewy and outsides crispy. The baking soda browns them evenly. Change up the flavors by skipping the salt and sprinkling with dried pizza spice, ranch seasoning, or Everything Bagel Seasoning.*

10 cups water
1 pound prepared pizza dough
1/2 cup baking soda

Egg wash (1 egg beaten with
 1 tablespoon water)
Coarse kosher salt

1. Spread several paper towels onto a work surface.

2. Bring water to a boil in a medium stockpot.

3. Meanwhile, divide the pizza dough in half and then into 8 to 10 smaller equal pieces.

4. Roll into ropes 1/4-inch thick and 6 to 8 inches long (depends on what size you want the pretzel, so adjust accordingly).

5. Make a U-shape with the rope and, holding the ends of the rope, cross them over each other and press onto the bottom of the U in order to form the shape of a pretzel. Set aside.

6. Preheat oven to 400°F.

7. When water is boiling, stir in the baking soda.

8. Gently lower a few pretzels at a time into the water for 25 seconds.

9. Flip them over and boil another 20 seconds. Transfer to paper towels and blot dry.

10. Place pretzels 1-inch apart onto a nonstick baking sheet.

11. Brush the egg wash over each pretzel, then sprinkle with salt.

12. Bake 15 to 20 minutes or until a deep golden brown.

13. Cool pretzels on a wire rack and store in an airtight container.

# roasted sweet potato wedges

## Makes: About 4 cups

*When cutting the potatoes, leave the skin on and cut them all the same size, so they bake evenly—and then dip away. These are tasty enough to serve as a little bite with a sprinkle of Parmesan cheese.*

4 small sweet potatoes,
 brushed clean
1 tablespoon olive oil

1 teaspoon garlic flakes
2 teaspoons dried Italian herb
 mix

1. Preheat oven to 450°F.

2. Cut potatoes into ½- to 1-inch wedges.

3. In a wide bowl, drizzle oil over the potatoes and add garlic and herbs. Toss to coat evenly.

4. Place wedges on a nonstick baking sheet in a single layer.

5. Bake for 20 minutes and then turn wedges over and bake another 5 minutes or until lightly browned and tender.

6. Serve warm or store in fridge and serve at room temp.

## Chapter 3

# little o'fares:
# finger foods and
# tea sandwiches

**To make the happy hour tea table more dramatic, mix and match** bite-sized foods. Create a menu that plays on an assortment of shapes, textures, and flavors. When you're planning, estimate four petite sandwiches per person. Any foods with mayo or other perishables should remain in the fridge until guests arrive.

You can set out a buffet-style spread with varying heights of plates such as a few three-tier tea caddies. Traditionally these tiered serving pieces were designed to accommodate high tea. The first course on top, main in the middle, and sweets on the bottom. Enough of these heavier hors d'oeuvres suggest the bounty of foods that might be served at a high tea, a teatime that usually replaces dinner, so you should advise your happy hour guests to come hungry.

# pick-me-ups

Cucumber Salad Stacks with Ranch Crema

Happy Hour Salad on a Stick

Stuffed Pinwheel Pop-Ups

Tea Bar Date Snacks

Marinated Roasted Peppers

Minty Watermelon Refresher

Devilishly Dolloped Eggs

Pizza Cupcakes

Herb-Crusted Salmon Whirls

Lil' Meatballs in Creamy Tea Sauce

Steak Rollups with Roasted Pepper Mayo

# cucumber salad stacks with ranch crema

## Makes: 8 (2-tier) stacks

*A short stack of greens is just right for a grab-and-eat teatime salad. Store any leftover ranch cream dressing or add more stacks. The little towers offer height to a teatime grazing board.*

¼ cup sour cream
½ cup mayonnaise
½ cup whipped cream cheese
2 tablespoons ranch seasoning blend
1 teaspoon finely chopped curly-leaf parsley

Salt and pepper to taste
1 large peeled cucumber, sliced into 16 (¼-inch thick) rounds
Baby arugula leaves
Peruvian pepper drops for garnish

1. With stand or hand mixer, cream together sour cream, mayonnaise, whipped cream cheese, ranch seasoning blend, and parsley to make a creamy, thick dressing.

2. Season with salt and pepper.

3. Cover and chill in fridge for two hours.

4. When ready to serve, build each stack with a dollop of cream and an arugula leaf between two cucumbers, ending with more spread on top and an arugula leaf overtop.

5. Drizzle lightly with a little more ranch spread and a pepper drop, or other small garnish of your choice.

# happy hour salad on a stick

Makes: 18 to 24 petite skewers

*Feel free to change out veggies as they are available, and switch out cheese with any other semi-hard varieties.*

3 tablespoons olive oil
1 tablespoon lemon zest
1 tablespoon lemon juice
1 tablespoon flat-leaf parsley
1 1/2 tablespoons dried oregano
8 ounces apple-smoked
   Cheddar cheese, diced small
24 small cherry tomatoes

1 small green or yellow bell
   pepper, cut into 1/2-inch
   pieces
8 ounces small white button
   mushrooms, stems removed
18 to 24 (4-inch) appetizer-size
   skewers such as knotted-end
   bamboo picks

1. Whisk together olive oil, lemon zest, lemon juice, parsley, and oregano.

2. Pour into an 8-inch square or a small rectangular casserole dish.

3. Thread the cheese, tomatoes, peppers, and mushrooms alternately as desired onto each skewer. Leave a little space at the top and bottom (do not over-thread) for handling.

4. Place into the casserole dish.

5. Cover and marinate in fridge for 2 to 4 hours, turning often on all sides.

# stuffed pinwheel pop-ups

## Makes: 18 pinwheels

*Food pinwheels are usually flat swirls but these have dimension and are not hard to make. Just keep the pastry chilled in the fridge while prepping, so the dough won't become limp and drag when cutting. If desired, push a thin, blunt wooden dowel into the pinwheel for convenient grab-and-eat. (If inserting before baking, soak sticks in water so they don't burn.)*

2 sheets puff pastry dough, thawed and lightly dusted with flour

1/3 cup pesto (such as basil, lemon-balm, kale)

1/2 cup finely chopped cooked (not to a crisp) bacon

1/3 cup finely chopped sundried tomatoes (not in oil)

Egg whites for egg wash

1/4 cup minced raw chopped almonds

1. Preheat oven to 400°F.

2. Line 3 baking sheets with parchment paper.

3. Unroll pastry.

4. Cut each into a rectangle, 10 x 15 inches (12 x 14 for smaller pinwheels).

5. Cut each sheet into 6 (4-inch) squares (into 10 or so 2½ inch squares for smaller pinwheels). The dough needs to be thin enough so the spokes of the pinwheel stay separated during baking.

6. Using the tip of a knife, make a slit from each corner to an inch of the center.

7. Dollop a tablespoon of the pesto into the centers. Then add bacon and tomatoes.

8. Fold each triangle into the center. Brush exposed dough with egg wash.

9. Sprinkle lightly with a little more filling and the nuts, but don't overfill.

10. Place on a sheet pan and bake each pan separately for 10 to 12 minutes or until golden brown. (Keep the other pans chilled in the freezer until they're ready to be baked.)

11. Let cool a few minutes before lifting off with a spatula and serving.

# tea bar date snacks

Makes: 24 servings

*There are many ways to stuff dates, but here, the caramel fruit flavor meets the smoky cheese and jam for a soft, chewy munch that pairs well with a cool cup of tea. It's best to work with Deglet Palm dates (readily available) because other dates are too large.*

24 pitted Deglet Palm dates
¼ cup or more Maple and
  Bacon Onion Jam (page 53)

4 ounces plain spreadable
  goat cheese
¼ cup or so assorted
  microgreens for garnish

1.  Slice dates in half lengthwise, but not all the way through.

2.  Open each date like a book and spread bacon jam inside.

3.  Dollop along the length of the date with goat cheese.

4.  Top with a few microgreens for garnish.

5.  Arrange dates, filling side up, on a serving plate.

# marinated roasted peppers

### Makes: About 2½ cups

*I keep these in the fridge (up to three weeks) for last-minute additions to appetizers or salads. They're also great on a cracker or bruschetta.*

3 large red bell peppers
½ cup olive oil, divided
2 small garlic cloves, minced
1 tablespoon balsamic vinegar

1 teaspoon dried Italian herbs
  of choice
Salt and cracked black pepper

1. Preheat oven to 425°F.

2. Cut peppers in half. Remove seeds and core.

3. Cut in half again and brush skins with a teaspoon of olive oil.

4. Place skin side up on a nonstick baking sheet and bake for at least 25 minutes or until skins blacken and peppers soften.

5. Remove peppers to a work surface and when cooled to handle, peel skin away with your fingers and discard.

6. Slice peppers thinly and add to a small storage container.

7. Stir in the vinegar, herbs, and remaining olive oil. Turn with a fork to mix, and season with salt and pepper.

# minty watermelon refresher

## Makes: 3 cups

*Healthy and colorful, keep this soothing treat handy
at your tea party as a palate cleanser.*

Zest from 1 lime
1/4 cup lime juice
1 tablespoon sugar
3 cups finely diced seedless
   watermelon
1 medium cucumber, peeled,
   seeded, and diced small

1/2 cup seeded and minced
   green bell pepper
2 tablespoons finely chopped
   fresh cilantro
2 tablespoons finely chopped
   fresh mint
1/4 teaspoon salt

1. In a large bowl, whisk the zest and lime juice with the sugar.

2. Add watermelon, cucumber, bell pepper, cilantro, and mint. Carefully turn to coat well.

3. Sprinkle with salt and serve.

note:
*Watermelon weeps its juice as it sits. If you're making this ahead, skip the salt until later and drain most of the liquid into a container. Reserve the liquid separately with the watermelon bowl covered in the fridge. When ready to serve, add the liquid back in and salt if desired.*

# devilishly dolloped eggs

Makes: 2 cups

*Instead of hard-boiled egg halves, carrot rounds hold a yummy filling. Castelvetrano green olives from Italy have the same buttery-sweet taste like traditional black olives.*

4 large eggs, hard-boiled and peeled
¼ cup mayonnaise
1 teaspoon Dijon mustard
½ small ripe avocado, mashed
¼ cup smoked salmon, finely chopped
½ teaspoon (or to taste) mushroom truffle powder
2 strips cooked bacon, finely chopped

2 tablespoons finely chopped pitted Castelvetrano or black olives
¼ cup roasted red peppers, finely chopped
½ cup coarsely grated Gruyere cheese
Salt and pepper
1 medium-large carrot, sliced into ¼-inch rounds

1. Slice eggs in half and add them to a large bowl, mashing them well.

2. Using a rubber spatula, mix (and smoothly mash) in mayonnaise, mustard, avocado, salmon, and truffle powder.

3. Fold in bacon, olives, peppers, and cheese.

4. Season to taste with the salt and pepper.

5. Scoop egg mixture onto each carrot round and serve.

# pizza cupcakes

## Makes: 16 servings

*Pizza is a popular party food. As a cupcake, it's dainty, less drippy, and manageable in one hand. If you make these ahead of time, you can pop them in the oven and warm before serving.*

1 can (8-count) dairy-case flaky biscuit dough
1/3 cup olive oil
1 1/2 cups shredded Mozzarella cheese
1 cup shredded sharp Provolone cheese
1/2 cup finely grated Pecorino Romano cheese
1 cup cooked ground mild Italian sausage, crumbled
3/4 cup minced red bell peppers
Olive oil for brushing

1. Preheat oven to 350ºF.

2. Cut each raw biscuit into quarters and place into a large mixing bowl.

3. Drizzle oil over the dough, mixing gently with a spatula to coat evenly.

4. Fold in the cheeses and then the sausage and the peppers.

5. Lightly brush 16 nonstick muffin cups with olive oil to encourage a golden, crispier crust.

6. Spoon in the biscuit-cheese mixture and bake 20 minutes or until tops are browning.

7. Release from pan and serve.

# herb-crusted salmon whirls

## Makes: 36 to 40 pieces

*Use a loaf of whole-wheat sliced bread, not the extra-wide, as the bread will be rolled out and made slightly larger anyway.*

16 slices whole-wheat bread, crusts removed
8 ounces whipped cream cheese
1½ teaspoons horseradish

½ cup chopped smoked salmon
¼ cup small capers
¼ cup green onion, minced
½ cup flat-leaf parsley, minced
¼ cup dill, finely chopped

1. Using a rolling pin, flatten bread and square off with a knife. Set aside.

2. In a small bowl, using a fork, combine cream cheese and horseradish.

3. Add in salmon, capers, and onions until smooth.

4. Evenly spread the mixture over each bread slice and cover to the edges.

5. Roll up each slice tightly.

6. Cut each roll crosswise into ½-inch thick slices.

7. Cover with plastic and chill for 2 hours.

8. When ready to serve, mix together parsley and dill and gently pat each rolled piece on one side into the herbs, and serve.

# lil' meatballs in creamy tea sauce

Makes: 24 mini meatballs

*Off the typical meatball-making grid are these round balls, moistened with spicy brewed tea. Keep in mind that tea is a great substitute ingredient for water (and in the case of meatballs, for milk too).*

3 tea bags such as ginger, chai, or gunpowder green
3/4 cup hot water
1 pound ground pork or pork/ beef mixture
1/4 cup plain breadcrumbs
2 cloves garlic, minced
1/2 teaspoon salt

3/4 cup crumbled feta cheese, divided
2 tablespoons olive oil
1 1/2 cups sour cream
1/2 teaspoon oregano
1/2 teaspoon black pepper
Chopped fresh parsley for sprinkling

1. Steep the tea bags in the hot water for 10 minutes. Discard and let tea cool.

2. In a large bowl, combine pork and breadcrumbs.

3. With your hands, add and combine garlic, salt, and 1/2 cup of the feta.

4. Pour in 2 to 3 tablespoons of the brewed tea, mixing well to moisten.

5. Roll meatballs into a tablespoon size, or use a small cookie scoop.

6. Heat the oil in a large skillet over medium heat and sauté the meatballs, turning to brown evenly. Transfer to a serving bowl.

7. Meanwhile, in a small saucepan over medium-low heat, melt the remaining feta with sour cream, oregano, pepper, and remaining tea.

8. Pour saucepan mixture over the meatballs. Sprinkle with parsley and serve.

# steak rollups with roasted pepper mayo

## Makes: 10 to 12 rollups

*Start a day ahead making the peppers and marinating the steak in your choice of a vinaigrette dressing and then broil to a medium-rare.*

3/4 cup mayonnaise
1/4 cup crème fraiche or thick
   Greek yogurt
3/4 cup marinated and drained
   roasted peppers (page 89)
1/2 cup soft Gorgonzola cheese

1/2 cup finely chopped flat-leaf
   parsley leaves
Salt and pepper
1 pound marinated flank steak,
   broiled
1 cup baby spinach or arugula

1. Place mayonnaise, crème fraiche, marinated and drained roasted peppers, Gorgonzola cheese, and parsley into a food processor.

2. Puree until smooth—30 seconds or so.

3. Season with salt and pepper.

4. Cut the steak angled against the grain into 1/4-inch slices.

5. Spread each slice with the roasted pepper mayo and add some spinach leaves.

6. Roll up each piece (optional to add a toothpick in each for easy handling) and place on a serving platter with extra mayonnaise for dipping.

# handhelds

⊱⊰

*To save room at the tea table, mix your cookies in with the sandwiches. Sandwiches with crusts represent a heartier, less-dainty option. Some cooks like to remove crusts after a sandwich is built. I prefer leaving crusts intact to prevent fillings from oozing out. If you'd like to go crustless, I recommend removing crusts first, and spreading the filling all the way out to the bread corners.*

*To make grabbing and holding on to sandwiches daintier and cleaner, keep fillings tucked inside, wrap the middle of the sandwiches in decorative paper, and secure with a ribbon or twine.*

Mashed Potato Spread on Tuna Sandwiches

Food Truck Zone Shrimp/Corn 'Wiches

Pimento Pita Pocket Poufs

Maple Leek and Brie Melts

Apple and Kraut Tea Cheese Rounds

Pineapple and Ham Sammies

# mashed potato spread on tuna sandwiches

### Makes: 16 tea sandwiches

*Mashed potatoes are a different spread option you can add to sandwiches.
Consider this spread when creating your own tea sandwiches.*

1 (5-ounce) can white albacore tuna, drained

½ cup mashed potatoes, seasoned with salt and pepper

2 tablespoons thick plain Greek yogurt

2 tablespoons minced green onions (white and green parts)

¼ cup finely minced dill pickles

8 slices dark sourdough bread or sprouted-grain bread

16 black pitted olives

16 small baby arugula leaves

1. In a medium bowl, flake the tuna and work in the potatoes and yogurt.

2. Fold in the onions and pickles and combine well.

3. Spread mixture onto four slices of the bread.

4. Top with the remaining bread slices.

5. Cut each sandwich into 4 triangles and secure with a toothpick impaled with an olive and arugula leaf.

# food truck zone shrimp/corn 'wiches

Makes: 12 sandwiches

*Shrimp, corn, and zucchini in a smoky cream is like the down-home melty fare you might find on a food truck these days. Make your favorite zucchini bread in a mini-loaf pan. I usually wrap these with mini flour tortillas, but for a tea, a sandwich tucks the goods neatly inside.*

2 tablespoons butter
12 medium fresh shrimp
Salt and pepper
1/2 to 3/4 cup corn kernels (about 1 cooked ear)
2 green onions, minced

1 1/2 tablespoons dried tarragon leaves
3 tablespoons crème fraiche or sour cream
1 teaspoon smoked paprika
12 slices mini-loaf pan zucchini bread

1. In a medium skillet, melt the butter over medium heat until foamy.

2. Toss in shrimp and cook for two minutes. Season with salt and pepper.

3. Stir in corn and cook for two additional minutes.

4. Turn in the onions and tarragon, and cook 30 seconds or until the flavors combine. Remove from heat and remove the shrimp from the mix.

5. Slice each shrimp in half lengthwise and set aside.

6. Stir the crème fraiche with paprika and then add to the corn mixture. Spread evenly onto half the bread slices.

7. Top with four shrimp halves and close the sandwiches with another slice of bread. Cut sandwiches in half and serve.

# pimento pita pocket poufs

Makes: 8 to 10 pita pockets

*Pimento cheese has all the flavor you need in this sandwich.
The celery gives it a crunch and the chives a tang. The cream
cheese helps soften and balance the peppery flavor.*

½ cup pimento cheese
2 tablespoons whipped cream
   cheese
2 tablespoons minced celery
1 tablespoon finely chopped
   fresh chives

1 cup finely diced cooked
   roasted chicken
1 teaspoon fresh chopped
   Italian-leaf parsley, plus
   more for garnish
8 mini (2½-inch) pita breads

1. Combine pimento cheese with cream cheese, celery, and chives.

2. Fold in the chicken and parsley.

3. Open pita pocket at the top with a knife and spread slightly. Fill each with the chicken mixture and serve.

# maple leek and brie melts

### Makes: 16 tea sandwiches

*Any cheese with Brie's buttery flavor and creamy texture
will do here. To slice Brie, turn the cheese wheel on its side,
cut off the rind and slice as per this sandwich.*

2 tablespoons butter, plus
  2 tablespoons melted
2 large leeks (white part only),
  cut lengthwise and then into
  1/4-inch slices

2 tablespoons maple syrup
1/3 cup water
8 slices country-style bread
4 slices (1/4-inch thick) ham
4 thick slices Brie cheese

1. In a small skillet, melt two tablespoons of the solid butter over medium heat and sauté the leeks for about three minutes until tender.

2. Turn heat down to a simmer, add the maple syrup and water, and cook two minutes until it's a gel consistency.

3. Place four slices of the bread on a work surface and evenly spread the maple-leek mixture evenly onto each slice.

4. Add ham and Brie.

5. Add remaining bread slices.

6. Brush both sides of the sandwiches with the melted butter.

7. Preheat a griddle pan and toast sandwiches, turning over once to melt the cheese.

8. Slice into four triangles each and serve.

# apple and kraut tea cheese rounds

Makes: 8 to 10 sandwiches

*These sandwiches literally make the rounds at happy hour!
They're great served on a grazing board. You can make the
powdered tea by grinding tea leaves finely in a nut grinder.*

1 loaf (16 slices) rye bread
½ teaspoon milk or heavy
   cream
3 ounces cream cheese
2 teaspoons powdered green
   or black tea of choice

1 small sweet, crisp apple such
   as Cosmic or Delicious
½ cup sauerkraut, drained
8 to 10 slices cooked bacon,
   cut in half

1. Using a 2½- inch biscuit cutter, stamp out bread slices for tops and bottoms. Set aside.

2. In a small bowl, mix milk with cream cheese.

3. Stir in tea powder. Combine well and spread on the rounds.

4. Cut the apple into ¼-inch thin slices, adding a slice to half of the rounds.

5. Mound sauerkraut overtop the apples, followed by bacon.

6. Close the sandwich with a top round and serve.

# pineapple and ham sammies

## Makes: Approximately 40 tea sandwiches

*Refreshing mint and pineapple with honey butter offer a
counterpoint in the mix of other rich-tasting tea party foods.*

2 slices deli ham (½-inch thick)
½ cup chopped fresh (or
   packaged and drained)
   pineapple
1 teaspoon Dijon-style mustard
Fresh cracked pepper
1 cup (2 sticks) butter, softened

2 tablespoons honey
2 tablespoons finely chopped
   fresh mint leaves, plus more
   to taste
20 thin slices whole-grain
   bread, crusts removed

1. In food processor, pulse and combine ham, pineapple, mustard, and a few cracks of pepper. Set aside.

2. In a small bowl, whisk together butter and honey and fold in mint.

3. Evenly spread the honey butter onto one side of all the bread slices (storing any leftover butter).

4. Add the pineapple mixture to half the slices.

5. Top with remaining bread (butter side in) and cut each into four squares or triangles.

# baked to a tea

"Hey, I'm ready," a whistling pot beckons from the stovetop. Echoing the nursery rhyme *"I'm a Little Teapot,"* the 1939 lyric sings about what happens when water reaches the boil: I get all steamed up! The rhyme cleverly teaches a childhood lesson about the workings of the teakettle always up to its nose (spout) in hot water and needing relief. "Tip me over and pour me out." It's also an endearing metaphor, reminding us of what to do when at our own tipping point. Pour it all out into a teacup and add to the calming influence with a sweet from one of our new or updated favorite tea recipes, or from our no-bake section, "Other Sweet Somethings."

# breads & scones

✦

Classic Scones

Chocolatey Yogurt Scones

Cranberry Ginger Bread

# classic scones

## Makes: 8 scones

*To easily change this up, omit the sugar and add grated cheese, onion powder, and herbs. To sweeten: whisk 1¼ cups powdered sugar, ½ cup maple syrup, and a dash of vanilla extract to make a glaze and drizzle overtop.*

2 cups all-purpose flour
⅓ cup sugar
1 tablespoon baking powder
½ teaspoon salt

¼ cup (½ stick) butter
1 egg
½ cup light cream, plus extra
   for brushing

1. Preheat oven to 425ºF.

2. In a large bowl, combine the flour, sugar, baking powder, and salt.

3. Using a pastry blender or two knives, cut in the butter until coarse crumbs form.

4. Add the egg and cream; stir to form a dough.

5. Transfer dough to a lightly floured surface, and knead for 1 minute.

6. With a floured rolling pin, roll dough out ½ inch thick.

7. Cut out scones with a 2-inch biscuit cutter. Place on a baking pan slightly apart, and brush tops lightly with the cream.

8. Bake 12 minutes or until golden brown.

# chocolatey yogurt scones

Makes: 12 scones

*Healthy yogurt allows for a fluffier scone by
balancing the leavening during baking.*

1½ cups all-purpose flour
½ teaspoon baking powder
½ teaspoon baking soda
⅛ teaspoon salt
3 tablespoons butter, chilled
   and cut into small pieces
1 cup finely chopped mixed
   dried fruits

½ cup toasted sunflower seeds
½ cup white chocolate chips
1 egg
½ cup plain yogurt
½ teaspoon grated lemon peel
6 teaspoons sugar

1. Preheat oven to 400ºF.

2. In a large bowl, combine the flour with the baking powder, baking soda, and salt.

3. Using a pastry blender or 2 knives, cut in the butter until coarse crumbs form.

4. Mix in the fruit, seeds, and chocolate; set aside.

5. In a medium bowl, whisk the egg with the yogurt, lemon peel, and sugar.

6. Whisk into the flour mixture, just to moisten and form a dough.

7. With wet hands, shape the dough into a round ball. Divide in half and roll each half to ½ inch thickness.

8. Using a 2-inch biscuit cutter, cut out scones and place onto a nonstick baking sheet slightly apart.

**9.** Bake 15 to 20 minutes or until golden brown.

**10.** Cool in pan on wire rack.

# cranberry ginger bread

## Makes: 1 loaf

*Buttery sweet, this popular tea bread can be complemented by cheese or crudites.*

1¼ cups all-purpose flour
1 teaspoon baking soda
½ teaspoon salt
1½ teaspoons cinnamon
1 egg, lightly beaten

1 cup milk
2 tablespoons butter, softened
1½ cups dried cranberries
¼ cup crystallized ginger
¾ cup sugar

1. Preheat oven to 375°F.

2. In a large mixing bowl, combine the flour, baking soda, salt, and cinnamon.

3. Add the egg, milk, and butter, mixing well to combine.

4. In a separate bowl, toss the cranberries and ginger with the sugar; fold into the flour mixture.

5. Turn the batter into a greased 9 x 5-inch loaf pan.

6. Bake 40 minutes or until the cake is golden brown.

7. Cool on a wire rack before turning out.

# cookies

Buttermint Cookies

Heartfelt Linzers

The All-In Cannoli Cookie (baked)

The Cannoli Sandwich Cookie (no-bake)

Tea-Zinged Sesame Cocktail Cookies

The Shortbread Tea Bag

Nutty Tea Snow Caps

Lemon Basil Cookies

Tea-Thyme Ginger Bars

Salted Toffee Chocolate Bark

Toasted Almond and Orange-Tea Biscotti

# buttermint cookies

Makes: 4 dozen

*Not too sweet, these are a classic refreshment for
happy hour with a little citrus zing.*

3/4 cup (1 1/2 sticks) butter
2/3 cup sugar
1 egg
1 teaspoon peppermint extract
1/2 teaspoon vanilla extract

1/2 teaspoon orange extract
2 cups all-purpose flour, sifted
2 tablespoons fresh mint
 leaves
Pinch of salt

1. Using a stand or hand mixer, cream the butter with the sugar until fluffy.

2. Beat in the egg and slowly add peppermint extract, vanilla extract, and orange extract.

3. Add flour, 1/2 cup at a time.

4. Add in mint and salt, beating until a dough forms.

5. Remove to a floured work surface and cut dough into 3 equal parts.

6. Shape each into a 1 1/4-inch thick log. Wrap in plastic and chill for 25 minutes.

7. Preheat oven to 350°F.

8. Cut the chilled dough into 1/4-inch thick rounds and arrange on 2 large nonstick baking sheets 1 inch apart.

9. Bake 10 to 12 minutes or until golden brown.

10. Cool pans on a wire rack for 5 minutes and then remove cookies to the rack to complete cooling.

# heartfelt linzers

## Makes: 2 dozen cookies

*Linzer sandwich cookies have that down-home cache. Though these are scalloped, you can use a round cutter. You'll need two hours to chill the dough.*

1¼ cups (2½ sticks) butter
1⅓ cups sugar, plus
  2 tablespoons
1 egg, plus 1 egg yolk
Grated peel of 1 medium
  lemon
3 cups all-purpose flour

1 teaspoon salt
3 teaspoons powdered green
  tea
1 cup finely ground almonds
1 cup finely ground walnuts
2 cups raspberry jam
Powdered sugar

1. Using a stand or hand mixer, cream butter and sugar until fluffy.

2. Add eggs and lemon peel; mix until blended.

3. Lower the speed and slowly add flour, salt, tea, and nuts, mixing just to form a dough.

4. Wrap in plastic and chill for 2 hours.

5. Preheat oven to 350°F.

6. On a lightly floured work surface, cut dough in half and roll a half out to ⅛-inch thickness.

7. Using a 2½-inch heart or other cookie cutter, cut out cookie bottoms and place on a nonstick baking sheet 1 inch apart.

8. Spread each with ½ teaspoon of jam to within ¼ inch from the edge.

9. Roll out remaining dough for tops, and cut the same way, using a smaller cutter to make the cookie windows.

10. Add tops to make a sandwich.

11. Bake 10 to 12 minutes or until golden brown.

12. Sprinkle with powdered sugar.

# the all-in cannoli cookie

## Makes: 2 dozen cookies

*Cannoli means "little tube," and in the Italian pastry by that name, it's a crisp-fried shell stuffed with flavored ricotta. Here are my two versions—one chocolatey with the essence of cannoli baked pillowy-soft into the dough (also known as a ricotta cookie), and the other with the filling freshly sandwiched between thin cookies. Both are lighter and daintier for a tea party.*

1 cup (2 sticks) butter, room
   temperature
1 cup sugar
1 egg, plus 1 egg yolk
1/2 cup ricotta cheese, drained
1 teaspoon almond extract
1 1/2 tablespoons orange-
   flavored Cointreau liqueur
1 1/2 teaspoons finely grated
   orange zest (about 1 orange)

2 cups all-purpose flour
1 1/2 teaspoons baking powder
1/2 teaspoon salt
3/4 cup mini chocolate chips
3/4 cup chopped unsalted
   pistachios
2 ounces dark chocolate,
   melted
White candy sprinkles,
   optional

1. Using a hand or stand mixer, cream butter and sugar until fluffy.

2. On low, beat in eggs, ricotta, almond extract, liqueur, and orange zest.

3. In a separate bowl mix flour, baking powder, and salt.

4. Add dry mixture to wet mixture, forming a dough. Blend well.

5. Fold in chocolate chips and nuts.

6. Wrap dough in plastic and chill for 1 hour.

7. Preheat oven to 350ºF.

8. Line 2 rimmed baking sheets with parchment paper.

9.  Drop 1½ rounded tablespoons of dough onto pans, 2 inches apart.

10. Bake 10 minutes or until golden brown on the edges.

11. Cool completely on a wire rack.

12. Melt chocolate and drizzle over top, and dot with sprinkles.

# the cannoli sandwich cookie

## Makes: 24 cookies

48 thin (2-inch round) cookies
3/4 cup ricotta cheese, drained
8 ounces mascarpone cheese
1/3 cup powdered sugar
3/4 teaspoon hazelnut extract

3/4 teaspoon orange extract
1/4 cup mini dark chocolate
chips, chopped
1/4 cup pistachio nuts, minced

1. Mix cheeses, powdered sugar, hazelnut extract, orange extract, chocolate chips, and pistachio nuts together and add to a pastry piping bag.

2. Pipe onto the underside of half the cookies.

3. Top with the remaining cookies and serve.

# tea-zinged sesame cocktail cookies

## Makes: 20 to 24 cookies

*My grandmother served these, but they weren't sweet enough for us kids. Now I love them because of that. Some of the changes I made are using light olive oil instead of butter, and using tea as a spice, which sets this cookie's character upright even with a glass of wine.*

½ cup raw sesame seeds
1½ cups all-purpose flour
½ cup stone-ground whole-wheat flour
1 teaspoon baking powder
½ teaspoon salt

½ cup sugar
2 teaspoons powdered chai tea
2 eggs
½ cup light olive oil
1 teaspoon vanilla extract

1. Preheat oven to 350ºF.

2. On a medium rimmed baking sheet, spread out the sesame seeds, and bake 10 minutes until golden (check to avoid burning); let cool.

3. In a large mixing bowl, whisk together all-purpose flour, whole-wheat flour, baking powder, salt, sugar, and tea; set aside.

4. Line two cookie sheets with parchment paper.

5. In a medium bowl, whisk the eggs with the oil and vanilla.

6. Pour into the dry ingredients and use a rubber spatula to mix until smooth (dough will be oily).

7. Using a level tablespoon, form each cookie into small logs 1½ inches long and ¾ inch thick.

8. Tamp each into the sesame seeds, covering completely.

9. Place cookies 1½ inches apart on the pans.

10. Bake 25 to 30 minutes or until firm and golden brown on the edges.

11. Cool a few minutes and then transfer cookies to a wire rack to cool completely.

Don't just
do something;
sit there.

- Thich Nhat Hanh

Deep Breath.

. . . .and exhale

# the shortbread tea bag

### Makes: 18 cookies

*Making these fun themed cookies takes a few steps, but it's a tea party hit—or send guests home with a cookie as a party favor. I recommend making the tea tags ahead of time.*

1/4 cup sugar
6 tablespoons butter, room temperature
3/4 cup, plus 1 tablespoon all-purpose flour
4 ounces semisweet chocolate pieces

1 (8 1/2 x 11-inch) sheet decorative craft or plain paper
Kitchen twine
Glue stick

## cookies

1. Cream together butter and sugar until fluffy; cut in the flour just until the dough comes together.

2. Roll dough into a ball, wrap in plastic, and chill 30 minutes.

3. Using a floured rolling pin and work surface, roll chilled dough into a 3/8-inch or so thick rectangle.

4. Cut dough strips 1 5/8 inches wide by 2 3/8 inches long.

5. Cut left and right corners on a diagonal (an actual tea bag can be your pattern).

6. Using the thin round of a pastry bag tip or a skewer, pierce a small hole 1/4 inch from the top center of cookie.

7. Place cookies on a sheet pan and chill for 30 minutes. Just before time is up, preheat oven to 350°F. Bake for 12 to 14 minutes until edges just turn golden.

8. Cool the pan on a wire rack for 2 minutes. Then remove cookies from pan and place on rack to cool completely.

## chocolate dip

1. Line a cookie sheet with parchment paper and set aside.

2. In a narrow container, microwave the chocolate, stirring every 20 to 30 seconds until melted.

3. Dip cookies a little less than halfway into the chocolate, let drip, and place on the parchment. Chill in pan for 15 minutes or until chocolate hardens.

## tea tag and assembly

1. Cut 18 pieces (10-inch long) thin twine or thread and set aside.

2. Cut 36 (1-inch) squares (2 per cookie); smear glue on the blank side of 18 squares (if paper is patterned).

3. Place a thread in the middle of the glued tag.

4. Press a second tag on top with the twine in between.

5. Carefully push the other end of the string through the cookie hole, pulling enough so that it measures 5 inches from top of the cookie to the tag.

6. Secure the thread in place by tying a knot. Snip off any excess.

# nutty tea snow caps

## Makes: 48 cookies

*It's not unusual to find cookies similar to these, providing*
*a tea table with a different shape and texture.*

2¼ cups all-purpose flour
¼ teaspoon salt
2 tablespoons powdered chai
   tea, plus more to sprinkle
1 cup (2 sticks) butter

½ cup powdered sugar, plus
   more for coating
1 teaspoon vanilla extract
¾ cup finely chopped pecans

1. Sift together the flour, salt, and tea; set aside.

2. Using a stand or hand mixer, cream together the butter, sugar, and vanilla until fluffy.

3. Gently add in the flour/tea mixture.

4. Fold in the pecans and form a dough; cover in plastic.

5. Chill for 2 hours.

6. Preheat oven to 400ºF.

7. Form dough into 1-inch balls and place on a nonstick cookie sheet; press down on each ball lightly for a flatter top, if desired.

8. Bake 10 to 12 minutes until set but not browned.

9. Cool slightly on a wire rack and then roll in the powdered sugar.

10. Return to rack and cool completely.

11. Roll in sugar again and sprinkle with a little of the powdered tea.

# lemon basil cookies

## Makes: 4 dozen

*Boxed cake mixes tend to make a softer texture for cookie baking.*

1/4 cup (1/2 stick) unsalted
   butter, room temperature
8 ounces cream cheese,
   softened
1 egg yolk
1 1/2 teaspoons grated lemon
   peel

1 teaspoon lemon juice
1 box lemon cake mix
1 1/4 cups golden raisins
1/2 cup finely chopped walnuts
3 tablespoons finely chopped
   basil leaves

1. Preheat oven to 350ºF.

2. Using a stand or hand mixer, cream together the butter, cream cheese, egg yolk, lemon peel, and juice until fluffy.

3. On low speed, slowly beat in the cake mix.

4. Fold in raisins, walnuts, and basil.

5. Drop by level teaspoon 1 inch apart onto a nonstick baking sheet.

6. Bake 15 to 18 minutes or until cookies are lightly browned.

# tea-thyme ginger bars

## Makes: 32 bars

*Peel the ginger and grate (might as well grate the entire knob for a cup of ginger tea!). Light oolong tea complements the ginger and the thyme flavors.*

**bars:**
- 2 cups all-purpose flour
- 1/2 teaspoon baking soda
- 1 tablespoon powdered ginger tea
- 1/8 teaspoon salt
- 1/2·cup golden raisins
- 3/4 cup (1 1/2 sticks) unsalted butter
- 3/4 cup packed brown sugar
- 1/2 cup dark molasses
- 1 egg
- 2 tablespoons finely grated ginger

**glaze:**
- 1 1/2 cups powdered sugar, sifted
- 2 tablespoons unsalted butter, melted
- 1 teaspoon pure vanilla extract
- 1/2 teaspoon grated orange peel
- 2 tablespoons orange juice
- Pinch of salt
- 2 generous teaspoons minced dried thyme leaves

1. Preheat oven to 350ºF.

2. Grease a 9x13-inch baking pan.

3. In a large bowl, combine the flour, baking soda, tea, and salt.

4. Fold in the raisins and set aside.

5. Using a stand or hand mixer, beat the butter, sugar, and molasses on medium speed for 2 minutes until fluffy.

6. Beat in the egg and ginger.

7. Reduce speed to low and slowly add in the flour/tea mixture until blended.

8. Spread the batter into the prepared pan and bake 25 minutes or until a tester comes out clean.

9. Transfer pan to a wire rack.

1. In a small bowl, whisk together the powdered sugar, butter, vanilla, orange peel and juice, salt, and thyme until smooth.

2. Spread over the slightly warm bars.

3. Cool completely before cutting into 8 long strips, and then crosswise into 4 bars each.

# salted toffee chocolate bark

## Makes: 1 sheet pan

*Toffee is roasted butter with caramelized sugar and when baked with salty crackers, the result is indescribable, so you just keep eating them. Optional: sprinkle the melted chocolate with 3/4 cup or so minced unsalted nuts.*

48 hard salty crackers, such as saltines
1 cup (2 sticks) butter
1 teaspoon vanilla extract

1½ cups packed brown sugar
¼ teaspoon salt
2 cups semisweet dark chocolate chips

1. Preheat oven to 350ºF.

2. Line a 9x15-inch baking sheet with aluminum foil.

3. Spread the crackers to cover the bottom of the pan and set aside.

4. In a small saucepan, melt the butter and stir in the vanilla extract, sugar, and salt.

5. Bring to a boil, then turn heat down and boil gently for 3 minutes.

6. Immediately pour the caramel mixture over the crackers, spreading it evenly with a spatula.

7. Bake in the oven 5 to 10 minutes or until bubbles start to form and edges begin to brown; remove and let rest 1 minute.

8. Generously sprinkle chocolate chips over the crackers, and as they melt, smooth the chocolate evenly over top the caramel.

9. Cool to room temperature about 10 minutes and then tent with foil (but not on the chocolate).

10. Chill overnight to harden.

11. Break into pieces to serve.

# toasted almond and orange-tea biscotti

## Makes: 28 to 30 biscotti

*Dip these cookies into a cup of hot tea or red wine. They won't get soggy on the way out of the cup and will leave behind a little flavor in the beverage!*

2³/₄ cups all-purpose flour
³/₄ cup sugar
Contents of 4 orange-spice
　tea bags
¹/₂ teaspoon allspice
1 tablespoon avocado oil

1 tablespoon Grand Marnier or
　orange juice
3 eggs, lightly beaten
1 teaspoon almond extract
¹/₂ cup sliced toasted almonds

1. Preheat oven to 350°F.

2. In a large bowl, combine the flour, sugar, tea, and allspice; set aside.

3. In a smaller bowl, mix the oil with the liqueur, eggs, and almond extract; add to the flour mixture.

4. Fold in the almonds, forming a dough (may be crumbly).

5. Turn dough out onto a floured work surface and knead lightly to smooth.

6. Divide in half, shaping each into an 8-inch loaf.

7. Place loaves 6 inches apart onto a nonstick baking sheet pan.

8. Using your palms, flatten each roll slightly.

9. Bake 30 minutes.

10. Remove the rolls from the pans to a wire rack to cool about 10 minutes.

11. Meanwhile, turn oven down to 325ºF.

12. Remove loaves to a work surface and cut each diagonally into 12 to 15 (¹/₂-inch) slices.

13. Place slices upright onto the baking pans and return pan to oven, baking another 8 to 12 minutes to harden.

14. Cool on a wire rack.

# cakes, pies, and muffins

Glazed Lemon Loaf Cake

Mocha Chocolate Brownie Cake

Tea-Kick Cake

Peachy Eat-It-With-a-Spooncake

Blueberry Vanilla Hand Pies

Buttermilk Butterscotchies

# glazed lemon loaf cake

## Makes: 1 loaf

*Yogurt added to cake creates a healthy leavening and a moist cake.*

1½ cups all-purpose flour
2 teaspoons baking powder
½ teaspoon salt
3 eggs
1 teaspoon vanilla extract
1 cup plain Greek yogurt
¾ cup sugar

2 tablespoons honey
Zest from 2 small lemons
  (reserve 1 teaspoon juice for
  the glaze)
½ cup light olive oil
2 cups powdered sugar

1. Preheat oven to 350ºF.

2. In a large bowl combine the flour with the baking powder and salt.

3. In a medium bowl, beat eggs and vanilla and lightly whisk in the yogurt, sugar, and honey.

4. Using a rubber spatula, turn in the lemon zest and oil, and add to the flour mixture, combining well.

5. Pour batter into a 9 x 5-inch nonstick loaf pan and bake 45 minutes or until golden brown on top.

6. Cool 10 minutes on a wire rack, then run a spatula around the edges; turn pan over and release the cake upright onto a plate.

7. Mix the reserved lemon juice with the powdered sugar and drizzle over top while cake is still a little warm.

8. Cool completely before slicing.

# mocha chocolate brownie cake

Makes: 1 (9-inch) cake

*Everything about the flavor comes up brownie,
but the texture is moister and cakier.*

1 cup (2 sticks) butter
3 cups sugar
4 eggs
1 cup sour cream
1/2 cup light olive oil
1/2 cup brewed coffee, chilled
3 cups all-purpose flour

1/2 teaspoon baking powder
1/2 teaspoon salt
1/2 cup unsweetened cocoa
  powder
1 cup mini chocolate chips
Powdered sugar
Shaved almonds, optional

1. Preheat oven to 325°F.

2. Using a stand or hand mixer, cream together the butter and sugar until smooth.

3. Beat in the eggs one at a time.

4. Beat in sour cream, oil, and coffee.

5. In another bowl, mix together the flour, baking powder, salt, and cocoa.

6. Fold in the chocolate chips.

7. Pour the batter into a greased and floured 9-inch square pan.

8. Bake 55 to 60 minutes or until a tester comes out clean.

9. Cool in the pan on a wire rack for about 10 minutes, then remove from the pan and let cool on the rack.

10. Sprinkle generously with powdered sugar and cut into squares as desired.

11. Garnish each square with shaved almonds, if desired.

# tea-kick cake

Makes: 8 to 10 servings

*When using a traditional layer cake recipe, skip the second layer. One layer is just the right size for a tea sweet.*

1½ cups all-purpose flour
½ teaspoon baking soda
2 teaspoons powdered ginger
   tea
1 teaspoon powdered chai tea
½ cup buttermilk
2 teaspoons vanilla extract

½ cup (1 stick) unsalted butter
½ cup packed light brown
   sugar
½ cup molasses
1 teaspoon grated orange peel
2 eggs
Chocolate frosting, optional

1. Preheat oven to 350°F.

2. Grease and flour a 9-inch square cake pan.

3. In a large bowl, whisk together the flour, baking soda, and powdered teas; set aside.

4. In a separate bowl, combine the buttermilk and vanilla; set aside.

5. Using a stand or hand mixer, cream together the butter and sugar until fluffy.

6. Beat in the molasses, orange peel, and eggs.

7. Add the flour mixture alternately with the buttermilk mixture, beating well after each addition.

8. Pour batter into the prepared pan.

9. Bake 35 to 40 minutes or until tester comes out clean.

10. Invert the cake onto a wire rack and cool completely.

11. Frost cake and cut into squares and serve.

# peachy eat-it-with-a-spooncake

## Makes: Approximately 16 small bowls

*Melt-in-your-mouth unfussy spooncake is so moist you eat it with a spoon. Made like a poke cake with the creamy ingredients of a tres leches, fruits such as peaches enhance the flavor and soft profile of spooncake, so I prefer them over chunky berries. For the tea party, you only need a taste, or, depending on the size of your party, you can serve more than the suggested amount.*

1 box yellow cake mix of choice
$\frac{1}{3}$ cup light olive oil
1 cup milk
3 eggs
5 medium-large peaches, peeled

3 tablespoons sugar
$\frac{1}{2}$ cup caramel sauce
1 (15-ounce) can sweetened condensed milk
1 cup evaporated milk

1.  Preheat oven to 350ºF.

2.  In a bowl, mix dry cake mix with the oil, milk, and eggs; set aside.

3.  Grease a 9 x 13-inch pan.

4.  Dice the peaches into 1-inch cubes, then evenly spread in pan and sprinkle with sugar; pour batter overtop.

5.  Bake 45 to 55 minutes until dark golden brown.

6.  Cool cake for 1 hour on a wire rack.

7.  Using the large end of a chopstick, poke holes in the cake, about 1-inch apart.

8.  Whisk the caramel sauce with the milks.

9.  Evenly pour over the cake and let absorb fully.

**10.** Serve warm or store in the fridge.

**note:**
*You can also replace the oil, milk, and eggs listed here with what your cake mix calls for, but use the baking instructions in this recipe, not on the box.*

# blueberry vanilla hand pies

Makes: 12 pies

*Half-moon-shaped turnovers are filled with ripe blueberries in these easy pies that fit in one hand while the other holds your teacup.*

3 ounces cream cheese, softened
6 tablespoons sugar, divided
½ teaspoon vanilla extract
2 egg yolks, divided
1 cup fresh blueberries
2 teaspoons cornstarch

2 teaspoons crème de cassis or black currant syrup
¼ teaspoon salt
3 sheets puff pastry, thawed but kept chilled
Powdered sugar

1. Combine cream cheese, 3 tablespoons sugar, vanilla, and 1 egg yolk in a medium bowl until smooth; set aside.

2. In a smaller bowl, toss the blueberries with the cornstarch, 2 tablespoons of the remaining sugar, the liqueur, and the salt; set aside.

3. Preheat oven to 375°F.

4. On a lightly floured surface, roll each pastry sheet into a 10-inch square.

5. Use a 4-inch round cutter to cut out 4 rounds of pastry from each sheet; arrange in 2 parchment-lined rimmed baking sheets.

6. Mix remaining yolk with a teaspoon of water and brush onto outer edge of rounds; dollop ½ tablespoon of the cream cheese mixture in the center of each.

7. Top rounds with 1 tablespoon of the blueberry mixture each.

8. Fold in half to form a half-moon, pinching edges to seal well (a little oozing is okay though).

9. Lightly brush pie tops with egg wash; sprinkle evenly with the remaining sugar.

10. With the tip of a knife, cut a couple of steam vents into the centers.

11. Bake 25 minutes or until golden brown.

12. Cool 3 minutes in pan, then transfer pies to wire rack.

13. Sprinkle with powdered sugar before serving.

# buttermilk butterscotchies

## Makes: 24 mini muffins

*You'll need an hour prep time to soften the oats. Use mini butterscotch chips, or coarsely chop larger ones. A delicious complement to a cup of Darjeeling tea.*

1 cup quick-cooking oats
1 cup buttermilk
Zest from 1 orange, divided
½ cup lightly packed light
  brown sugar
1 cup all-purpose flour
1 teaspoon baking powder
½ teaspoon baking soda

½ teaspoon salt
1/3 cup butter, melted and
  cooled
1 egg, beaten
2 tablespoons honey
½ cup mini butterscotch chips
Powdered sugar

1. In a medium bowl, mix together oats, buttermilk, and half the orange zest.

2. Sprinkle sugar overtop; let sit an hour.

3. Preheat oven to 400°F.

4. In a separate bowl, sift the flour with the baking powder, baking soda, and salt; set aside.

5. Combine the butter, egg, and honey with the oat mixture.

6. Add the flour mixture, stirring gently, just to incorporate.

7. Fold in the butterscotch chips.

8. Spoon the batter 3/4 full into greased mini muffin cups. Sprinkle with remaining orange zest.

9. Bake 8 to 10 minutes or until golden.

10. Cool on a wire rack.

11. Sprinkle with powdered sugar and serve.

# other sweet somethings

Caramel Apple Muffin Twirl

Potato Chip Walnut Tartlets

Almond Truffles

Apricot Rum Riot Dessert Tea

Puddle-of-Chocolate and Chai Pots de Crème

Sweet Lemon Sauce

Teasicles

# caramel apple muffin twirl

## Makes: 6 servings

*Easier to eat than a caramel apple, and adding a lot of pizzazz
to the tea table, this sweet looks like a rose but smells like
an apple pie, and it packs the same homey punch!*

2 red apples such as Gala,
   Jazz, Pippin (cored)
2 tablespoons lemon juice
3 tablespoons apple jam

2 tablespoons quality caramel
   sauce, plus more for plating
1 sheet puff pastry, thawed
Cinnamon sugar for sprinkling
1 cup vanilla bean ice cream

1. Cut apples in half and slice paper-thin.

2. Place apple slices in a microwave-safe bowl covered with water and the lemon juice.

3. Microwave 2 to 3 minutes until tender (not mushy); drain and pat dry.

4. Cover with plastic wrap and a tea towel to keep soft; set aside.

5. Mix the apple jam with caramel sauce; set aside.

6. On a floured surface, roll out the pastry about 1/8-inch thick.

7. Cut into 6 even and straight strips.

8. Preheat oven to 375°F.

9. Brush each strip lightly with the caramel mixture.

10. Start placing apple slices 1/4-inch off the end, slightly overlapping and each piece extending just past the edge of the dough.

11. Sprinkle apples lightly with cinnamon sugar.

12. Fold the dough up ⅔ of the way to cover bottom of the apples, pressing down lightly to hold each apple in place.

13. Roll from one end to the next and place each flower into nonstick muffin tin cups.

14. Bake 25 minutes and remove from oven.

15. Quickly sprinkle tops with cinnamon sugar and return to oven, baking another 10 to 15 minutes or until golden brown (be careful not to burn edges).

16. Cool on wire rack and remove when still slightly warm.

17. To serve, melt the ice cream and pool on individual plates, topping with the muffin twirl.

# potato chip walnut tartlets

## Makes: 24 mini tarts

*Salty sweets are in, so now when I make this family recipe, I add chips to tamp the sweet and up the yummy. A simple cream cheese dough forms a crust baked in a muffin tin with a nutty candied filling and a crunchy chip topping.*

**pastry cups:**
1/4 cup (1/2 stick) butter
3 ounces cream cheese,
  softened
1 cup sifted all-purpose flour

**filling:**
3/4 cup dark brown sugar
1/4 teaspoon salt
1 egg, slightly beaten
1 teaspoon vanilla extract
1 tablespoon butter
2/3 cup finely chopped walnuts
3/4 cup coarsely crushed
  potato chips

1. Combine the half stick of butter and cream cheese.

2. Add the flour and form a dough.

3. Preheat oven to 350°F.

4. Roll out the dough to 1/8 inch thick.

5. Line each cup of a mini muffin tin with small pieces of the dough, pressing against the sides and up to the top of the cup; set aside.

6. Mix together sugar, salt, egg, vanilla, and 1 tablespoon of the butter.

7. Fold in the walnuts.

8. Fill the muffin cups to the top and bake 20 minutes or until pastry cups are golden brown.

**9.** As soon as tarts come out of the oven, immediately sprinkle tops with the chips so it hardens into a salty candied crunch.

**10.** Cool on a wire rack a few minutes before running a rubber spatula around the edges and popping out the tarts.

# almond truffles

### Makes: 4 dozen truffles

*Energy bars move over, the latest are these delicious afternoon
pick-me-ups wrapped up into a ball and coated with coconut.*

1½ cups old-fashioned oats
¾ cup almond butter or tahini
¼ cup honey
½ teaspoon salt
3 tablespoons mixed flax and
   chia seeds

½ cup finely chopped almonds
¾ cup mini chocolate chips
½ cup finely shredded
   unsweetened coconut, or
   more if needed

1. In the bowl of a food processor, pulse the oats, tahini, honey, salt, and
   seeds several times, scraping down the sides of the bowl.

2. Fold in the almonds and chocolate chips.

3. Working with wet hands, roll the mixture into balls, using 1 tablespoon
   mix per ball.

4. Roll in the coconut.

5. Refrigerate until ready to serve.

# apricot rum riot dessert tea

## Makes: 6 servings

*Serving this in brandy snifters offers a soothing
finish to the happy hour teatime.*

1 cup water
2 teaspoons sugar
2 Orange Pekoe tea bags
2 tablespoons minced dried
  orange peel

2 cups apricot nectar
Light rum
Grand Marnier
Sparkling water, optional

1.  Combine water, sugar, tea bags, and orange peel in a small saucepan
    and simmer on medium-low for 10 minutes; remove from heat and let
    steep for 15 minutes.

2.  Remove tea bags and stir in the apricot nectar.

3.  Cool down and transfer to a pitcher. Chill in fridge until ready to serve.

4.  Evenly divide into 6 medium brandy snifter glasses; add ice and a
    splash each of the liqueur and rum.

5.  Fill the rest of the glass with sparkling water, if bubbly essence is
    desired.

# puddle-of-chocolate and chai pots de crème

## Makes: 2 to 4 small cups

*Serve with a smear of whipped cream or crème fraiche. A little thicker with more avocado and this makes a nice icing for tea cakes.*

1¼ cups avocado flesh (½ of a Florida avocado or 2 smaller avocados)

½ cup honey, plus more for tasting

⅓ cup unsweetened cacao powder

½ cup unsweetened coconut milk (not coconut water)

1 tablespoon vanilla extract

2 teaspoons powdered chai tea, plus more for sprinkling

1. In food processor, whirl together the avocado and ½ cup honey.

2. Add cacao, coconut milk, and vanilla; whirl on low to combine, about 30 seconds.

3. Scrape the sides of the bowl and taste, adding more honey if desired.

4. Add the tea and whirl another 30 seconds or until smooth.

5. Serve in individual cups. Top with whipped cream and a sprinkle of the chai tea, if desired.

# sweet lemon sauce

## Makes: 3 cups

*When you want to switch up a recipe, this is an easy add-on that has a dramatic effect. Top it on sweet breads, puddle it under cupcakes and muffins, pour it over fruits and ice cream. Or if you're up for it, stir a little into your teacup!*

2 cups water
1 cup sugar
2 tablespoons cornstarch
¼ cup (½ stick) butter

2 tablespoons grated lemon peel
¼ cup fresh lemon juice

1. Add water to a 2-quart saucepan.

2. Stir in the sugar and cornstarch, bringing the mixture to a boil.

3. Stir on medium-high heat for 5 to 6 minutes until sugar is dissolved and sauce thickens.

4. Stir in lemon peel, lemon juice, and butter.

5. Let cool 30 minutes prior to serving or store in the fridge.

# teasicles

Makes: Depends on mold sizes

*The size of the molds used for larger pops and the type of ice cube trays
for the smaller ones can make anywhere from 10 to a couple dozen.
The flavors dilute when frozen, so taste the liquid before molding,
and adjust with sweeteners. To make smaller teasicles, freeze in tiny
ice cube trays for an hour, then push small popsicle sticks upright
into the middle of each cube. Freeze for another hour until solid.
Here are four different flavors to try:*

## berry hibiscus

4 cups water
6 hibiscus tea bags
1/2 cup (or more) sweetener of
  choice

2 strawberries, sliced (finely
chopped for the ice cube
pops)

1. Bring the water to a boil in a saucepan or teakettle.

2. Add the tea bags and remove from heat and steep 15 minutes.

3. Stir in the sweetener, tasting to adjust.

4. Pour tea mixture into molds, adding berry slices into each.

5. Place in freezer and let sit overnight or until fully frozen.

# lavender mint

4 cups water
6 Earl Grey tea bags
1/2 cup (or more) sweetener of
    choice

1/4 teaspoon lavender
1/4 teaspoon mint extract
1/2 cup milk
1/2 cup cream

1. Bring the water to a boil in a saucepan or teakettle.

2. Add the tea bags and remove from heat and steep 15 minutes.

3. Stir in the sweetener, tasting to adjust.

4. Add lavender and mint extract, milk, and cream.

5. Pour into molds and freeze.

# coconut matcha

1. Blend $\frac{1}{2}$ cup milk and $\frac{1}{2}$ cup heavy cream with 1 can (13 ounces) coconut milk, 2 teaspoons matcha tea powder, and $\frac{1}{2}$ cup sweetener.

2. Pour into molds and freeze.

# lemon peppermint

1. Add $\frac{1}{4}$ cup honey to 4 cups lightly steeped peppermint tea, 3 tablespoons lemon juice, and $\frac{1}{4}$ teaspoon lemon extract.

2. Pour into molds and freeze.

# acknowledgments

I was inspired to write this book after I found a teatime puzzle, designed by Korean artist Yoon Jung Lee, in my neighborhood lending library. Perhaps the puzzle was telling me, "Draw yourself a cup of tea and—like the 1,000 pieces here—all things will fall into place."

Thank you to my sister, Dot. You braved my challenge to design a cookie tea bag and nailed it with your attention to detail. You also gave me your thumbs up—well, actually your talented thumbs down—since that's what thumbprint cookies need to become scoops.

That same can-do spirit came from Bonita Gragg who baked the blackberry lattice pie.

Imaginative cook Dawn Sullivan helped develop a few recipes with me—including the spooncake with white peaches gifted to me by Tom Lowe of Brushy Mountain Orchards in Moravian Falls, North Carolina. John Sullivan, who crafts the tea grazing boards for Dawn to paint, rigged the miniature clothesline I had in mind to clearly show the array of tea bag shapes. I do believe that this book is the first ever to demo tea bags in this way! Also a great way to dry used tea bags, especially when needed in a recipe.

Although ice pops made with tea are not new, calling them teasicles is. I leaned on the expertise of Maddie Warner for complementary happy hour tea ice-pop recipes. Farmer by day, fashionista model by night—she was the perfect source for these sweet pops and palate cleansers, since she also runs an entire business on pops, *Poppies*.

I also want to recognize other tea devotees, who inspire me through their must-read books: *Harney & Sons Guide to Tea* by Michael Harney, *For All the Tea in China* page-turner by Sarah Rose, and *Darjeeling: The Colorful History and Precarious Fate of the World's Greatest Tea* by Jeff Koehler. Thank you to my tea mentor, John Harney. When I think of tea's charm, sway, and effect, Harneyisms come to mind as John was a tea evangelist. And to the bed-and-breakfast innkeepers. I've written a lot about afternoon tea as happy hour, a welcoming event every day at hundreds of B&Bs and country inns. I'm happy to see that trends show that teatime as happy hour has gone mainstream.

And finally for my loving husband, Tom, who has more strength and stability than any person I've ever known. Thank you for your enduring patience and bonhomie spirit. You've supported my efforts to live the can-do life ever since the poem *A Heap O' Livin'* by Edgar Guest was shared with me by my high school classmate.

> Can't is a word that is foe to ambition,
> An enemy ambush to shatter your will;
> Its prey forever a man with a mission
> And bows only to courage, and patience, and skill.
> So hate it with hatred that's deep and undying,
> For once it is welcomed, 'twill break any man;
> And whatever the goal you are seeking, keep trying!
> And answer this demon by saying, "I Can!"

As I put this book together, I also completed the puzzle, which was satisfying on both fronts. And so, for whoever placed it in that library, I have something to leave in return—a copy of this book with my gratitude!

And to you, the tea drinker! I hope my recipes will become teatime favorites for you.

# about the author

Inspired by teas and new ways to serve them, Gail Greco wrote and photographed the recipes in this third book on tea, after *Tea Time Journeys* and *Tea Time at the Inn*. A two-time award-winning news journalist, she also writes about food and home lifestyles. She has authored sixteen cookbooks, plus edited and produced many for chefs, organizations, and home cooks. She wrote, directed, and produced hundreds of original social media recipe videos for DuPont Non-Stick Cookware Surfaces and for Boar's Head Deli Provisions. She was executive food editor for the Discovery Channel's *World Class Cuisine* TV series where she advanced her cooking craft under the world's top chefs. Gail was executive producer and host of her own PBS TV series, *Country Inn Cooking with Gail Greco*, which won a James Beard Best TV Food Journalism award. She was East Coast field editor of *Romantic Homes Magazine* and has written for national publications including *Country Home, Coastal Living, and Victorian Homes*. She has taught journalism at State University of New York. With one hand on the keyboard and with the other holding a teacup, she works by the balmy Gulf waters of southwest Florida and on a mountain peak in western North Carolina.

# index

## A

Alcohol
    Apricot Rum Riot Dessert Tea, 168
    Chilled Wine Tea, 31
    Lemony Cream Sherry Iced Tea, 23
    Rum Raisin Cheddar Spread, 60
    Spiked Peach and Coconut Tea Grog, 32
    Tea Toddy One-Shot, 35
Alice's Sorbet Float Tea recipe, 26
The All-In Cannoli Cookie recipe, 126–127
Almond Truffles recipe, 167
Apple and Kraut Tea Cheese Rounds recipe, 109
Apple Hibiscus Tea recipe, 11
Apricot Rum Riot Dessert Tea recipe, 168
Aristotle, x

## B

Bacon
    Apple and Kraut Tea Cheese Rounds, 109
    Buffalo Hot Chicken Dip, 41
    Devilishly Dolloped Eggs, 93
    Maple and Bacon Onion Jam, 53
    Stuffed Pinwheel Pop-Ups, 84–85
Baked Mushroom Patè recipe, 62–63
Baked Ricotta Dip recipe, 42
Basic Barista Tea Latte with Rooibos recipe, 16
Black tea
    Apple and Kraut Tea Cheese Rounds, 109
    Salted Caramel Cold Brew Milk Tea, 27
    Tea Toddy One-Shot, 35
Blueberry Vanilla Hand Pies recipe, 156–157
Boiling, xii–xiii
Breads and Scones
    Chocolately Yogurt Scones, 118–119
    Classic Scones, 117
    Cranberry Ginger Bread, 120
Brewing, xii–xiii
Buffalo Hot Chicken Dip recipe, 41
Buttermilk Butterscotchies recipe, 158–159
Buttermint Cookies recipe, 123

## C

Cakes
    Glazed Lemon Loaf Cake, 148
    Mocha Chocolate Brownie Cake, 150–151
    Peachy Eat-It-with-a-Spooncake, 154–155
    Tea-Kick Cake, 152–153
The Cannoli Sandwich Cookie recipe, 129
Caramel Apple Muffin Twirl recipe, 162–163
Chai tea
    Puddle-of-Chocolate and Chai Pots de Crème, 171
    Tea-Kick Cake, 152–153
    Tea-Zinged Sesame Cocktail Cookies, 130–131
Cheddar Ranch Crab Dip recipe, 46
Cheese
    The All-In Cannoli Cookie, 126–127
    Apple and Kraut Tea Cheese Rounds, 109
    Baked Mushroom Patè, 62–63
    Baked Ricotta Dip, 42
    Blueberry Vanilla Hand Pies, 156–157
    Buffalo Hot Chicken Dip, 41
    The Cannoli Sandwich Cookie, 129
    Cheddar Ranch Crab Dip, 46
    Cucumber Salad Stacks with Ranch Crema, 80
    Happy Hour Salad on a Stick, 83
    Herb-Crusted Salmon Whirls, 96
    Lemon Basil Cookies, 138
    Lemony Smoked Trout, 47
    Lil' Meatballs in Creamy Tea Sauce, 97
    Maple Leek and Brie Melts, 108
    Pimento Pita Pocket Poufs, 107
    Pizza Cupcakes, 94
    Potato Chip Walnut Tartlets, 164–165
    Ranch-Style Cucumber Spread, 61
    Rum Raisin Cheddar Spread, 60
    Savory Thumbprint Cookie Cups, 68–69
    Steak Rollups with Roasted Pepper Mayo, 98
    Sundried Tomato Creamy Cheese, 64
    Tea Bar Date Snacks, 86
    Toasted Walnut Microgreens Pesto, 59
    Whipped Feta Dip, 45

Chilled Wine Tea recipe, 31
Chocolate
    The All-In Cannoli Cookie, 126–127
    Almond Truffles, 167
    The Cannoli Sandwich Cookie, 129
    Chocolately Yogurt Scones, 118–119
    Chocolate Mint and Coconut Tea Latte, 18
    Mocha Chocolate Brownie Cake, 150–151
    Puddle-of-Chocolate and Chai Pots de Crème, 171
    Salted Toffee Chocolate Bark, 142–143
    The Shortbread Tea Bag, 133–134
Chocolately Yogurt Scones recipe, 118–119
Chocolate Mint and Coconut Tea Latte recipe, 18
Classic Scones recipe, 117
Coconut Matcha Teasicle recipe, 174
Cold Brews, Iced Teas, and Cool Spirits
    Alice's Sorbet Float Tea, 26
    Chilled Wine Tea, 31
    Fruity Herbal Iced Tea Sparkler, 24
    Happy Hour Muddled-Mint Tea Cocktail, 28
    Lemony Cream Sherry Iced Tea, 23
    overview of, 21
    Salted Caramel Cold Brew Milk Tea, 27
    Spiked Peach and Coconut Tea Grog, 32
    Tea Toddy One-Shot, 35
Cookies
    The All-In Cannoli Cookie, 126–127
    Buttermint Cookies, 123
    The Cannoli Sandwich Cookie, 129
    Heartfelt Linzers, 124–125
    Lemon Basil Cookies, 138
    Nutty Tea Snow Caps, 136
    Salted Toffee Chocolate Bark, 142–143
    The Shortbread Tea Bag, 133–134
    Tea-Thyme Ginger Bars, 139–140
    Tea-Zinged Sesame Cocktail Cookies, 130–131
    Toasted Almond and Orange-Tea Biscotti, 144–145
Cooking with tea, xxi
Cranberry Ginger Bread recipe, 120
Cucumber Salad Stacks with Ranch Crema recipe, 80

## D

Desserts
    The All-In Cannoli Cookie, 126–127
    Almond Truffles, 167
    Apricot Rum Riot Dessert Tea, 168
    Blueberry Vanilla Hand Pies, 156–157
    Buttermilk Butterscotchies, 158–159
    Buttermint Cookies, 123
    The Cannoli Sandwich Cookie, 129
    Caramel Apple Muffin Twirl, 162–163
    Coconut Matcha Teasicle, 174
    Glazed Lemon Loaf Cake, 148
    Heartfelt Linzers, 124–125
    Lavender Mint Teasicle, 174
    Lemon Basil Cookies, 138
    Lemon Peppermint Teasicle, 174
    Mocha Chocolate Brownie Cake, 150–151
    Nutty Tea Snow Caps, 136
    Peachy Eat-It-with-a-Spooncake, 154–155
    Potato Chip Walnut Tartlets, 164–165
    Puddle-of-Chocolate and Chai Pots de Crème, 171
    Salted Toffee Chocolate Bark, 142–143
    The Shortbread Tea Bag, 133–134
    Sweet Lemon Sauce, 172
    Tea-Kick Cake, 152–153
    Teasicles, 173
    Tea-Thyme Ginger Bars, 139–140
    Tea-Zinged Sesame Cocktail Cookies, 130–131
    Toasted Almond and Orange-Tea Biscotti, 144–145
Devilishly Dolloped Eggs recipe, 93
Dips
    Baked Ricotta Dip, 42
    Buffalo Hot Chicken Dip, 41
    Cheddar Ranch Crab Dip, 46
    Lemony Smoked Trout, 47
    Spicy Baked Artichoke Bruschetta, 40
    Whipped Feta Dip, 45
    White Bean "Hummus," 48

## E

Earl Grey Vanilla Almond Milk Latte recipe, 17

## F

Finger Food
    Cucumber Salad Stacks with Ranch Crema, 80
    Devilishly Dolloped Eggs, 93
    Happy Hour Salad on a Stick, 83
    Herb-Crusted Salmon Whirls, 96
    Lil' Meatballs in Creamy Tea Sauce, 97
    Marinated Roasted Peppers, 89
    Minty Watermelon Refresher, 90
    Pizza Cupcakes, 94
    Steak Rollups with Roasted Pepper Mayo, 98

Stuffed Pinwheel Pop-Ups, 84–85
Tea Bar Date Snacks, 86
Five O'clock High Tea Mockteal recipe, 15
Food Truck Zone Shrimp/Corn 'Wiches recipe, 104
French press coffee and teamaker, xv
Fruit
    Almond Truffles, 167
    Apple and Kraut Tea Cheese Rounds, 109
    Apricot Rum Riot Dessert Tea, 168
    Blueberry Vanilla Hand Pies, 156–157
    Caramel Apple Muffin Twirl, 162–163
    Cranberry Ginger Bread, 120
    Fruity Herbal Iced Tea Sparkler, 24
    Happy Hour Muddled-Mint Tea Cocktail, 28
    Lemon Basil Cookies, 138
    Minty Watermelon Refresher, 90
    Peachy Eat-It-with-a-Spooncake,
        154–155
    Pineapple and Ham Sammies, 110
    Red Cherry Relish, 57
    Rum Raisin Cheddar Spread, 60
    Spiked Peach and Coconut Tea Grog, 32
    Tea Bar Date Snacks, 86
    Teasicles, 173
    Tea-Thyme Ginger Bars, 139–140
Fruity Herbal Iced Tea Sparkler recipe, 24

## G

Ginger Date Tea recipe, 12
Glazed Lemon Loaf Cake recipe, 148
Grazing board, 37
Green tea
    Apple and Kraut Tea Cheese Rounds, 109
    Heartfelt Linzers, 124–125
    Savory Thumbprint Cookie Cups, 68–69

## H

Handhelds
    Food Truck Zone Shrimp/Corn 'Wiches, 104
    Maple Leek and Brie Melts, 108
    Mashed Potato Spread on Tuna Sandwiches, 102
    overview of, 101
    Pimento Pita Pocket Poufs, 107
    Pineapple and Ham Sammies, 110
Happy Hour Muddled-Mint Tea Cocktail recipe, 28
Happy Hour Salad on a Stick, 83
Happy Hour Tea, ix
Heartfelt Linzers recipe, 124–125

Herb-Crusted Salmon Whirls recipe, 96
Herbs
    Baked Ricotta Dip, 42
    Marinated Roasted Peppers, 89
    Minty Watermelon Refresher, 90
    Roasted Delicata Squash Dippers, 70
    Roasted Sweet Potato Wedges, 75
    tea blend from, 1, xx
    Tea-Thyme Ginger Bars, 139–140
Hibiscus tea
    Apple Hibiscus Tea, 11
    Happy Hour Muddled-Mint Tea Cocktail, 28
    Teasicles, 173
Honey, 4
Hot teas
    Apple Hibiscus Tea, 11
    Basic Barista Tea Latte with Rooibos, 16
    Chocolate Mint and Coconut Tea Latte, 18
    Earl Grey Vanilla Almond Milk Latte, 17
    Five O'clock High Tea Mockteal, 15
    Ginger Date Tea, 12
    overview of, 9

## J

Juice
    Apple Hibiscus Tea, 11
    Caramel Apple Muffin Twirl, 162–163
    Fruity Herbal Iced Tea Sparkler, 24
    Happy Hour Muddled-Mint Tea Cocktail, 28
    Toasted Almond and Orange-Tea Biscotti, 144–145

## K

Kombucha tea, 2

## L

Lapsang Souchong tea, xxii
Lavender Mint Teasicle recipe, 174
Lemon Aioli recipe, 54
Lemon Basil Cookies recipe, 138
Lemon Peppermint Teasicle recipe, 174
Lemons
    as add-in, 3
    Fruity Herbal Iced Tea Sparkler, 24
    Glazed Lemon Loaf Cake, 148
    Lemon Aioli, 54
    Lemon Basil Cookies, 138
    Lemon Peppermint Teasicle, 174
    Lemony Cream Sherry Iced Tea, 23

Lemony Cream Sherry Iced Tea recipe, 23
Lemony Smoked Trout recipe, 47
Lil' Meatballs in Creamy Tea Sauce recipe, 97

## M
Maple and Bacon Onion Jam recipe, 53
Maple Leek and Brie Melts recipe, 108
Marinated Roasted Peppers recipe, 89
Marshmallows, 4
Mashed Potato Spread on Tuna Sandwiches recipe, 102
Matcha tea, 2
Meat
    Apple and Kraut Tea Cheese Rounds, 109
    Buffalo Hot Chicken Dip, 41
    Cheddar Ranch Crab Dip, 46
    Devilishly Dolloped Eggs, 93
    Food Truck Zone Shrimp/Corn 'Wiches, 104
    Herb-Crusted Salmon Whirls, 96
    Lemony Smoked Trout, 47
    Lil' Meatballs in Creamy Tea Sauce, 97
    Maple and Bacon Onion Jam, 53
    Maple Leek and Brie Melts, 108
    Mashed Potato Spread on Tuna Sandwiches, 102
    Pimento Pita Pocket Poufs, 107
    Pineapple and Ham Sammies, 110
    Pizza Cupcakes, 94
    Steak Rollups with Roasted Pepper Mayo, 98
    Stuffed Pinwheel Pop-Ups, 84–85
Mini Soft Baked Pretzels recipe, 72–73
Minty Watermelon Refresher recipe, 90
Mocha Chocolate Brownie Cake recipe, 150–151

## N
Nuts
    The All-In Cannoli Cookie, 126–127
    Almond Truffles, 167
    The Cannoli Sandwich Cookie, 129
    Heartfelt Linzers, 124–125
    Lemon Basil Cookies, 138
    Nutty Tea Snow Caps, 136
    Potato Chip Walnut Tartlets, 164–165
    Toasted Almond and Orange-Tea Biscotti, 144–145
    Toasted Walnut Microgreens Pesto, 59
Nutty Tea Snow Caps recipe, 136

## P
Peachy Eat-It-with-a-Spooncake recipe, 154–155
Peppermint tea

Chocolate Mint and Coconut Tea Latte, 18
Lemon Peppermint Teasicle, 174
overview of, 2
Pick-Me-Ups
    Cucumber Salad Stacks with Ranch Crema, 80
    Devilishly Dolloped Eggs, 93
    Happy Hour Salad on a Stick, 83
    Herb-Crusted Salmon Whirls, 96
    Lil' Meatballs in Creamy Tea Sauce, 97
    Marinated Roasted Peppers, 89
    Minty Watermelon Refresher, 90
    Pizza Cupcakes, 94
    Steak Rollups with Roasted Pepper Mayo, 98
    Stuffed Pinwheel Pop-Ups, 84–85
    Tea Bar Date Snacks, 86
Pimento Pita Pocket Poufs recipe, 107
Pineapple and Ham Sammies recipe, 110
Pizza Cupcakes recipe, 94
Potato Chip Walnut Tartlets recipe, 164–165
Pour-over process, xv
Puddle-of-Chocolate and Chai Pots de Crème recipe, 171

## R
Ranch-Style Cucumber Spread recipe, 61
Red Cherry Relish recipe, 57
Roasted Delicata Squash Dippers recipe, 70
Roasted Sweet Potato Wedges recipe, 75
Rum Raisin Cheddar Spread recipe, 60

## S
Salted Caramel Cold Brew Milk Tea recipe, 27
Salted Toffee Chocolate Bark recipe, 142–143
Savory Thumbprint Cookie Cups recipe, 68–69
Scoops
    Mini Soft Baked Pretzels, 72–73
    Roasted Delicata Squash Dippers, 70
    Roasted Sweet Potato Wedges, 75
    Savory Thumbprint Cookie Cups, 68–69
Seafood
    Cheddar Ranch Crab Dip, 46
    Devilishly Dolloped Eggs, 93
    Food Truck Zone Shrimp/Corn 'Wiches, 104
    Herb-Crusted Salmon Whirls, 96
    Lemony Smoked Trout, 47
    Mashed Potato Spread on Tuna Sandwiches, 102
The Shortbread Tea Bag recipe, 133–134
Smoked tea, xxii

Spicy Baked Artichoke Bruschetta recipe, 40
Spiked Peach and Coconut Tea Grog recipe, 32
Spreads
    Baked Mushroom Patè, 62–63
    Lemon Aioli, 54
    Maple and Bacon Onion Jam, 53
    Ranch-Style Cucumber Spread, 61
    Red Cherry Relish, 57
    Rum Raisin Cheddar Spread, 60
    Sundried Tomato Creamy Cheese, 64
    Toasted Walnut Microgreens Pesto, 59
Steak Rollups with Roasted Pepper Mayo recipe, 98
Steeping, xii–xiii, xix
Stuffed Pinwheel Pop-Ups recipe, 84–85
Sundried Tomato Creamy Cheese recipe, 64
Sweeteners, 4
Sweet Lemon Sauce recipe, 172

## T

Tea
    Alice's Sorbet Float Tea, 26
    Apple Hibiscus Tea, 11
    Apricot Rum Riot Dessert Tea, 168
    Basic Barista Tea Latte with Rooibos, 16
    Chilled Wine Tea, 31
    Chocolate Mint and Coconut Tea Latte, 18
    cooking with, xxi
    Earl Grey Vanilla Almond Milk Latte, 17
    Five O'clock High Tea Mockteal, 15
    Fruity Herbal Iced Tea Sparkler, 24
    Ginger Date Tea, 12
    Happy Hour Muddled-Mint Tea Cocktail, 28
    Kombucha tea, 2
    Lapsang Souchong tea, xxii
    Lemony Cream Sherry Iced Tea, 23
    Matcha tea, 2
    overview of, 9, 21
    Peppermint tea, 2
    Salted Caramel Cold Brew Milk Tea, 27
    Smoked tea, xxii
    Spiked Peach and Coconut Tea Grog, 32
    Tea Toddy One-Shot, 35
    Yerba mate, 2
Tea, benefits and sources of, x, 1
Tea bags, xix
Tea Bar Date Snacks recipe, 86

Tea blend, creating, xx
Teacups, 7
Teakettle, xii–xiii
Tea-Kick Cake recipe, 152–153
Tea leaves, xvi, xxi, xxii
Teapot, xii
Teasicles recipe, 173
Tea strainer, xvi
Tea-Thyme Ginger Bars recipe, 139–140
Tea Toddy One-Shot recipe, 35
Tea-Zinged Sesame Cocktail Cookies recipe, 130–131
Thich Nhat Hanh, x
Toasted Almond and Orange-Tea Biscotti recipe, 144–145
Toasted Walnut Microgreens Pesto recipe, 59

## V

Vegetables
    Baked Mushroom Pate, 62–63
    Cucumber Salad Stacks with Ranch Crema, 80
    Devilishly Dolloped Eggs, 93
    Food Truck Zone Shrimp/Corn 'Wiches, 104
    Happy Hour Salad on a Stick, 83
    Herb-Crusted Salmon Whirls, 96
    Maple and Bacon Onion Jam, 53
    Marinated Roasted Peppers, 89
    Mashed Potato Spread on Tuna Sandwiches, 102
    Minty Watermelon Refresher, 90
    Pizza Cupcakes, 94
    Ranch-Style Cucumber Spread, 61
    Roasted Delicata Squash Dippers, 70
    Roasted Sweet Potato Wedges, 75
    Spicy Baked Artichoke Bruschetta, 40
    Steak Rollups with Roasted Pepper Mayo, 98
    Stuffed Pinwheel Pop-Ups, 84–85
    Sundried Tomato Creamy Cheese, 64
    Toasted Walnut Microgreens Pesto, 59
    Whipped Feta Dip, 45

## W

Whipped Feta Dip recipe, 45
White Bean "Hummus" recipe, 48

## Y

Yerba mate, 2